THE ATLANTIC CRITICAL STUDIES

ERNEST HEMINGWAY'S

The Old Man and the Sea

P.G. Rama Rao

ATLANTIC

PUBLISHERS & DISTRIBUTORS (P) LTD

Published by

ATLANTIC

PUBLISHERS & DISTRIBUTORS (P) LTD

7/22, Ansari Road, Darya Ganj, New Delhi-110002
Phones : +91-11-40775252, 40775214, 23273880, 23275880
Fax: +91-11-23285873
Web: www.atlanticbooks.com
E-mail: orders@atlanticbooks.com

Reprint 2012, 2017, 2021, 2022, 2023

Printed & bound in India by Atlantic Print Services

General Preface

The Atlantic Critical Studies are study-aids modelled on the study-aids available in England and America, among other places, and are primarily meant for the students of English Literature of Indian universities.

However, in consideration of the local conditions and the various constraints under which our students have to study—non-availability of relevant critical books, dearth of foreign and Indian journals, inaccessibility to good, well-equipped libraries, just to mention a few of them—the models have been considerably improved upon, both qualitatively and quantitatively.

Thus, while these studies are meant to be comprehensive and self-sufficient, the distinguished scholars who have prepared these study materials, have taken special care to combine lucidity and profundity in their treatment of the texts.

The Select Bibliography at the end is meant not only to acknowledge the sources used but also to help a student in the pursuit of further studies if s/he wants to.

Atlantic Publishers & Distributors (P) Ltd., believe in quality and excellence. These studies will only reconfirm it.

MOHIT K. RAY
Chief Editor [English Literature]
Atlantic Publishers & Distributors (P) Ltd.,
New Delhi

Preface

I am beholden to Dr. K.R. Gupta and Dr. Mohit K. Roy for asking me to write critical studies of Hemingway's *The Old Man and the Sea.*

In the late 1960s I wrote my Ph.D. Thesis on "The Narrative Technique of Ernest Hemingway" at the American Studies Research Centre, Hyderabad, where I was a Research Fellow in 1968 and 1969. One of my earlier books is based on my research, which was published by S. Chand & Company Ltd., New Delhi, and released at the All India English Teachers' Conference, Madras, in December 1979. I studied the Hemingway manuscripts in the John F. Kennedy Presidential Library, Boston; the New York Public Library; the Newberry Library, Chicago; the H.R.C. Library, Austin (Texas); the Bancroft Library, Berkeley (Cal); and the Library of Congress, Washington DC in 1981-82. Since most of the Hemingway papers are in the Kennedy Library, I spent most of that year in Boston, where I was a Fulbright Adjunct Professor in the Department of English, University of Massachusetts, Boston.

I had the privilege of meeting Charles Scribner Jr., Malcolm Cowley, Alfred Rice and other Associates of Hemingway, participating in the Hemingway Conference in Harvard Club, New York, and meeting leading Hemingway scholars there, and in the MLA Conference. Later, I attended the Second International Hemingway Conference at Lignano Sabbiadoro (Italy), and acted as Rapporteur in June 1986. In June 1988 I participated in the Third International Hemingway Conference at Schruns (Austria) and presented papers in two sessions.

I lectured on Hemingway in the English Department, Edinburgh University, in October 1986 during my visit to the Oxford and Edinburgh Universities as a British Council Visitor. In 1993 I visited the U.S.A. on a Fulbright American

Research Fellowship and studied the manuscripts of the posthumously published novel, *The Garden of Eden*. I was again an Adjunct Professor in the American Studies Department of the University of Massachusetts, Boston, where I lectured on the revisions in the manuscripts of *The Garden of Eden*. In October 1993 I made a lecture tour of several universities in the U.S.A. and Canada [University of Vermont, University of Puget Sound, Tacoma, (WA); the New School of Social Sciences, New York; Reed College, Portland (Oregon); and the University of British Columbia, Vancouver (Canada)].

After my retirement from Utkal University, Bhubaneswar (Orissa) in February 1995, I acted as a Visiting Fellow at the American Studies Research Centre, Hyderabad, where I organized a National Seminar on 'Hemingway and Film' in November 1995.

Having involved myself with Hemingway studies for nearly four decades, writing and lecturing on him, I was delighted when I was asked to write the critical study on *The Old Man and the Sea*.

Unlike some contemporary Hemingway scholars, I consider *The Old Man and the Sea* one of Hemingway's best works, if not the best of his works. I have tried to study this novella against the background of his total work published during his lifetime. This gives us a proper perspective. A study in isolation of this novella, torn out of the total creative output of the author gives us a lopsided view of the novel, its themes, characters, techniques and meanings.

The important thing for us to consider is not why Hemingway wrote, what he wrote, but how he wrote it, for a writer writes from his experience and the reader shares that experience. It would be unfair to find fault with a writer for writing about certain things and not writing about certain other things for he has the freedom to choose his subjects like any of us.

If I have succeeded in arousing the interest of the reader well enough to make him read this novella in depth and enjoy the experience, I have not written in vain.

P.G. RAMA RAO

Contents

1

A Celebrated Writer

> Veteran out of the wars before he was twenty:
> Famous at twenty-five: thirty a master—
> Whittled a style for his time from a walnut stick,
> In a carpenter's loft in a street of the April city.
>
> (Archibald Macleish on Hemingway)

It was the last week of January 1954. Ernest Hemingway, the celebrated American writer, sat in a corner room in Lake Victoria Hotel at Entebbe, Uganda, reading with great pleasure and amusement the obituaries in all the newspapers of the world as well as hundreds of glowing tributes from prominent people in the world. The whole world thought that he was dead. He and Mary had just survived two air-crashes. Hemingway's injuries included a full-scale concussion, a ruptured liver, spleen and kidney, temporary loss of vision in the left eye, loss of hearing in the left ear, a crushed vertebra, a sprained right arm and shoulder, a sprained left leg, and bad burns on his face, arms and head. Lying in his bed, he told newsmen that he had never been better. *Il faut durer* (we must endure) was his motto.

What did he look like? In Carlos Baker's words, "one's first impression of him was of size and strength. He was six feet tall and usually weighed about 210 pounds. He had a tendency to put on weight and was once up to 260 pounds.... His eyes were brown, his complexion ruddy, and there were dimples in both his cheeks which his beard later concealed..." (Carlos Baker, *Ernest Hemingway: A Life Story*, 3-4).

He loved outdoor activities and manly sports. Fishing and bullfighting were the two great passions in his life; boxing and big game hunting came next. He believed in the aesthetics of truthful writing. "...I found the greatest difficulty, aside from knowing truly what you really felt, rather than what you were supposed to feel, and had been taught to feel, was to put down what really happened in action; what the actual things were which produced the emotion that you experienced" (*Death in the Afternoon*, 10).

Hemingway had already won the Pulitzer Prize and it was widely believed that he would be awarded the Nobel Prize sooner or later. In fact, he won the Nobel Prize nine months later. Along with William Faulkner, who was already a Nobel Laureate, he was the tallest writer of his time.

2

A Brief Life-Sketch

Ernest Hemingway was born on July 21, 1899 at Oak Park, Illinois. He was the second of six children—four daughters and two sons—born to Dr. Clarence Edmonds Hemingway and Grace Hall Hemingway. Clarence was a physician and naturalist while Grace was a contralto and voice teacher.

He attended the Oak Park High School during 1913-17. After completing High School he moved to Kansas city where he worked on the staff of *Kansas City Star* as a cub reporter for six months. In 1917, he wanted to join the army but was disqualified because of his weak left eye and joined the Italian Red Cross Ambulance Corps in 1918. The Austro-Italian war was going on at that time and Hemingway's assignment was at Fossalta, a heavily damaged village near the river Piave. Here on July 8, 1918, he was severely wounded in both the legs by a trench mortar while carrying a supply of cigarettes, chocolate and postcards for the soldiers. Close to him was a man more severely wounded and piteously crying for help. In spite of his own severe wounds, Ernest carried the wounded man towards the command post before losing consciousness. Three years later he was honoured with Italy's *Medaglia d'Argento al Valore Militare* and *Croce ad Merito di Guerra.*

He recuperated in the Red Cross Hospital in Milan, where he fell in love with one of the nurses called Agnes Von Kurowsky. He returned to Oak Park as a wounded war hero in 1919. Rejected by Agnes, he started writing fiction.

In 1920, he moved to Toronto and wrote for *The Toronto Star Weekly*. Later he travelled to Chicago where he met two famous writers—Sherwood Anderson, the fiction-writer, and Carl Sandburg, the poet.

In September 1921, he married Hadley Chase and in December, sailed with her for Paris as European correspondent for *The Toronto Star Weekly*. In 1922, they set up house in Latin Quarter in Paris and met well-known writers like Gertrude Stein, Ezra Pound, John Dos Passos, James Joyce, and Ford Madox Ford. Later, Hemingway covered the Greco-Turkish war in Constantinople and the conferences in Geneva and Lausanne. Hadley left Paris to join her husband in Lausanne. On the way she lost the valise containing all of Hemingway's manuscripts.

In 1923, Hemingway travelled to Spain to see bullfights for the first time. This was the beginning of a lifelong affair with Spain and bullfights. The year 1923 saw the publication of his first book, *Three Stories and Ten Poems* (Contact editions), and the birth of his first child, John Hadley "Bumby" Nicanor Hemingway, endearingly referred to as Bumby in Toronto.

The Hemingways returned to Paris from Toronto in 1924, and Hemingway joined Ford Madox Ford's *Transatlantic Review* as Associate Editor. His literary circle was much larger now and he started getting noticed as a writer.

Boni and Liveright published Hemingway's first major work, *In Our Time*, in 1925. He met Pauline Pfeiffer, a staffer of the Paris edition of *Vogue* magazine, whom he was to marry two years later, and the famous American writer, F. Scott Fitzgerald, with whom he developed a close friendship. He visited Pamplona with family and friends in the same year and got the inspiration and material for his novel *The Sun Also Rises*.

Hemingway wrote a novel titled *The Torrents of Spring*, in which he parodied the style of Sherwood Anderson, and sent the manuscript to Boni and Liveright for publication. Boni and Liveright rejected the manuscript as it made fun of their leading author. The rejection nullified the contract and freed Hemingway to seek another publisher. Charles Scribner's sons published it and *The Sun Also Rises* in 1926 and all of Hemingway's subsequent works.

Hemingway married Pauline Pfeiffer in May 1927 after his divorce from Hadley Chase. In the same year he published *Men without Women.*

The year 1928 was an eventful year. He began writing *A Farewell to Arms* based on his experiences as a Red Cross Ambulance driver in Italy during the Austro-Italian war. After the birth of his second son, Patrick, by caesarian section, he got the material to conclude *A Farewell to Arms* (which was to be published in 1929). In 1928, he moved to Key West, Florida, and began ocean-fishing. His father committed suicide in December.

He met with a car accident in October 1930 and spent eight weeks in a hospital in Billings, Montana. Pauline's uncle bought the Key West home as a gift for her in 1931. Hemingway's third son, Gregory Hancock Hemingway was born in November of the same year.

His *Death in the Afternoon,* a treatise on bullfighting, which includes his views on the craft of writing and his aesthetic principles, was published in 1932. He began marlin-fishing in the same year and caught fifty marlins in two months in 1933. He published *Winner Take Nothing*, his third story collection in 1933. He went on an African safari with Pauline in 1933.

In 1935, Hemingway published *Green Hills of Africa*, a fictionalized account of his African safari. The year 1936 saw the publication of two of his most anthologized stories, *The Snows of Kilimanjaro* and *The Short Happy Life of Francis Macomber.*

He went to Spain in 1937 as a war correspondent to cover the Spanish Civil War for the North Atlantic Newspapers Association (NANA). He published his third novel, *To Have and Have Not* and his only play, *The Fifth Column.*

In 1940, he divorced Pauline and married Martha Gell Horn, a fellow journalist whom he had met in Spain. He also published *For Whom The Bell Tolls*, his fourth novel, based on the Spanish Civil War. He visited China with Martha in 1941.

He made Havana, Cuba, his home, where he lived at Finca Vigia ('Lookout Farm'), and patrolled the North Coast of Cuba, in his fishing boat, Pilar, looking for Nazi submarines in 1942, with the approval of the Government of the U.S.A.

In 1944, he went to England and Europe as war correspondent for Collier's to cover the Second World War with the Fourth Infantry of the army of the U.S.A. In London, he met Mary Welsh, who was writing for the London Bureau of *Time, Life* and *Fortune* magazines. He divorced Martha and married Mary in March 1946. He was working off and on on *Islands in the Stream* and *The Garden of Eden* during this period.

In 1948, he travelled to Italy, where he met the beautiful Adriana Ivancich, who inspired *Across the River and into the Trees* and the character of Renata.

Across the River and into the Trees, his fifth novel, was published in 1950. This novel was adversely reviewed and Hemingway's health also was poor at this time.

There was a sudden spurt in his fortunes in 1952 with the publication of *The Old Man and the Sea*, his sixth novel, in *Life* magazine. He won the Pulitzer Prize in 1953 and travelled to Spain to watch the bullfights which he did not see for over two decades. After that, in 1954 he went with Mary on an African safari and suffered two air-crashes in quick succession. He and Mary were believed to be dead and he had the unique privilege of knowing what the world thought of him as a man and as a writer by reading the obituaries and the tributes in the newspapers and magazines. He suffered serious burns, multiple injuries and a concussion and could not attend the Awards ceremony in Stolkholm, when he won the Nobel Prize for Literature. In 1955 and 1956, he assisted in filming *The Old Man and the Sea.* Hemingway's *The Dangerous Summer*, a non-fiction account of bullfighting "duel" was serialized in *Life* magazine in 1960. He suffered from depression, delusions and paranoia and was admitted to the Mayo clinic in Rochester, Minnesota, where he was given electric shock therapy.

In 1961, he was discharged from Mayo clinic and returned to Ketchum, Idaho, but had to be readmitted there owing to suicidal depression. After two months, he returned to Ketchum and killed himself with his shotgun on July 2, 1961.

A Moveable Feast (1964), *Islands in the Stream* (1970), *The Garden of Eden* (1986), and *True at First Light* (1999) were all published posthumously. There is still a lot of unpublished material in the Hemingway Room of The John F. Kennedy Presidential Library in Boston, and it will not be a surprise if more posthumous works are published in future.

3

The Making of a Writer

The writer in Hemingway was born during 1915-16 when his stories were published in *Tabula*, his school's literary magazine, and his byline in *Trapeze*, the weekly paper of his school. In 1917, he joined the *Kansas City Star* as a journalist. The *Star*'s famous style sheet, which included instructions like "Use short sentences", "Never use old slang", and "Avoid the use of adjectives", especially such extravagant ones as *splendid, gorgeous, grand, magnificent* etc., eventually led to the famous style which he honed for himself later with its well-known verbal economy, the declarative sentences, and the avoidance of unnecessary adjectives and adverbs.

The traumatic shock he suffered when he was seriously wounded at Fossalta di Piave on July 8, 1918, marked the turning point in his life and writing career resulting in what is called in psychological terms a "repetitive compulsion" and an obsession with the theme of death and violence.

Even after his physical wounds healed, the psychic wound refused to go away, and stayed with him and in his writings for the rest of his life.

Hemingway left with Hadley for Paris as a roving correspondent for the Toronto *Star Weekly,* armed with letters of introduction from Sherwood Anderson, who had just returned from Europe. It was in Europe that he turned from journalism to creative writing. His work as a journalist for four years was an invaluable training in the craft of fiction writing. His eye for the dramatic moment and the *mot juste* can be seen in this sentence from his report on the Lausanne

Conference in 1922: "The hall is crowded and sweltering and the four empty chairs of the Soviet delegation are the four emptiest looking chairs I have ever seen." His verbal economy in his cryptic dispatch on his interview with Kemal Pasha points to the famous understatement in his fiction: "Kemal inswards unburned Smyrna Guilty Greeks." The cable was decoded as "Mustapha Kemal in an exclusive interview today with the correspondent of the Monumental News Service denied vehemently that the Turkish forces had any part in the burning of Smyrna. The city, Kemal stated, was fired by incendiaries in the troops of the Greek rearguard before the first Turkish patrols entered the city." In Paris, he read the great continental writers in Sylvia Beach's book shop, "Shakespeare and Company", learnt from painting, Cezanne in particular, and, above all, from Gertrude Stein and Ezra Pound. Stein's advice, "Begin over again and concentrate" after reading his manuscripts, proved prophetic when Hadley lost all his manuscripts while traveling from Paris to Lausanne.

In Sylvia Beach's book shop, he went through an intensive course in reading prose-masters like Turgenev, Chekhov, Tolstoy, Dostoevski, Stendhal, Balzac, Flaubert and James Joyce. It was here that he occasionally met T.S. Eliot, Wyndham Lewis, Ford Madox Ford, and James Joyce. His future work was to show traces of the influence of Eliot and Joyce.

Hemingway learnt much from painting and music too. He told Lillian Ross in the celebrated *New Yorker* interview: "I learned to write by looking at paintings in the Luxembourg Museum in Paris" (35). He learned much from music, especially from Bach: "In the first paragraph of 'Farewell'(sic), I used the word 'and' consciously over and over the way Mr. Johann Sebastian Bach used a note in music when he was emitting counterpoint" (Sylvia Beach, 88).

It is difficult to say that Hemingway learnt only from writers like Stein, Pound and Eliot, painters like Cezanne and musicians like Bach. He kept his eyes and ears and, above all, his mind open, and learnt from all his experiences, from his discussions with the writers, artists, and journalists he moved with.

The *Bible* is another influence on his prose. Charles Fenton tells us that he told Samuel Putnam in an interview, that took place shortly after the publication of *The Sun Also Rises* in 1925, that he learnt to write by reading the *Bible*, particularly, *The Old Testament* (16).

Hemingway's first important work of fiction was *In Our Time* (1925), a remarkably innovative and novel achievement in short story writing with sharp vignettes on real life incidents alternating with short fictions written in tight, simple and limpid prose. In 1926, he made fun of Sherwood Anderson, the most celebrated writer at that time, through a parody called *The Torrents of Spring*, published by Charles Scribner's Sons, who published all his subsequent works.

His next work, *The Sun Also Rises*, which appeared as *Fiesta* in England (1926), a story of the post-war generation with its moral degradation and promiscuity, made waves in the literary world with its tight, clipped writing, the kind of which had never been written before, and the unobtrusive craftsmanship proving the adage that art lies in concealing art. The well-known sobriquet, 'The Lost Generation' came from one of the two epigraphs to this novel. The action moves back and forth between France and Spain, two of the three countries he loved most (the third being Italy). The Third International Hemingway Conference was held at Schruns (Austria), where he had revised the first draft of *The Sun Also Rises*, in June 1988 (the first at Madrid and the second at Lignano, Italy). I was pleasantly surprised to see a Hemingway museum at Madlener Haus (which hosted a lunch for us, the delegates) on the slopes of an Alpine skiing resort.

He published *Men without Women*, his second collection of short stories in 1927, and, curiously enough, he was divorced from Hadley in the same year and married Pauline Pfeiffer.

A Farewell to Arms (1929), one of Hemingway's most popular novels and one of the best novels on love and war ever written in English, established a firm reputation for Hemingway as one of the foremost writers of fiction in the English speaking world. It is the poignant story of an American ambulance driver in the Italian army, who is deeply in love with an English nurse, and is disillusioned with war and bids farewell to arms in the hope of finding comfort in the arms of love but soon finds himself bidding farewell to those arms also. The novel is based on Hemingway's own experience in the Austro-Italian war.

The delegates to the Second International Hemingway Conference in June 1986 at Lignano on the Adriatic, of whom I was one, were profoundly moved by the way Italy still honoured the memory of Hemingway. There is a memorial for him at Fossalta di Piave, where he was wounded in 1918. We were given civic receptions in five cities; the Italian aristocracy played host to us in four villas, and the Italian army held an unforgettable reception for us—with army band and all pomp and ceremony. All this was in homage to the memory of Hemingway.

He published his third collection of short stories, *Winner Take Nothing* in 1930, and his treatise on bullfighting, *Death in the Afternoon*, which also contains some of his aesthetic convictions in 1932. Hemingway and Pauline went on an African safari, for four months in 1933, which resulted in the first ever Non-Fiction Novel, *Green Hills of Africa* (1933), written about three decades before Norman Mailer and Truman Capote made the genre popular, and two great short stories, "The Snows of Kilimanjaro" and "The Short Happy Life of Francis Macomber".

The African safari marks the turning point in Hemingway's world view and his themes and techniques. The protagonist, who wanted to make a separate peace in the first two novels, articulates the need for team work and solidarity towards the end of his third novel, *To Have and Have Not* (1937), when Harry Morgan dies with the words, "No matter how a man alone ain't got no bloody chance", on his lips. The narrative perspective changes from the first person to the third person reflecting the shift from the individual to the collective viewpoint and action. The ironic tone of the early novels gives way to the use of paradox as a framework in the manner of Jesus's and Donne's paradoxes.

His fourth collection of stories together with his only play, *The Fifth Column,* appeared as *The Fifth Column and the First Forty-Nine Stories* (1938). Hemingway's experiments with the shifting of the narrative perspective in *To Have and Have Not* led to a more artistic use of the technique in his next novel, *For Whom the Bell Tolls* (1940), a novel of epic proportions, which presents the guerilla action against Franco's forces in the Spanish civil war, and the Spanish ethos. It is another great novel on war and love.

In *Across the River and into the Trees* (1950), the protagonist, Col. Cantwell, returns to his beloved city, Venice, before his death. In most of this novel, the narrative focus is on a single character and his perspective. This technique is put to the best use in *The Old Man and the Sea* (1952), in which an old fisherman goes far out in the sea to catch the biggest fish, the kind of which no fisherman ever caught before, and catches a huge marlin after a three-day struggle only to lose most of it to the sharks after a bitter fight. Hemingway believes that if a writer knows what he is writing about and is writing truly enough, he may omit things that he knows and the reader will have a feeling of those things as strongly as though the writer had stated them. He says in *Death in the Afternoon*: "The dignity of movement of an iceberg is due to only one-eighth of it being above water."

Hemingway won the Pulitzer Prize in 1953, and the Nobel Prize for Literature in 1954 for "his powerful style-making mastery of the art of modern narration". He did not attend the ceremonies in Stockholm but sent an acceptance message, which presents his literary credo in a nutshell. All his novels and many of his short stories have been filmed and interpreted again and again from various angles by scholars and critics. Of the four major posthumous publications, *The Garden of Eden* (1986) aroused a great deal of critical discussion. Part of the controversy is due to the liberties taken by the editors with the manuscript—the omissions and the commissions.

Hemingway became a legend in his lifetime and his eventful and colourful life ended on July 2, 1961, after a spell of paranoia and delusions. He had led an active outdoor life amid violence and pain most of the time, seen three wars from a close range, sometimes as an insider, and written some of the finest prose of our time and called himself a 'champ'. His personality is beautifully captured by a *Newyorker* cartoon in the 1930s, which shows a brawny, muscle-knotted forearm and a hairy hand clutching a rose, entitled "The Soul of Ernest Hemingway".

4

Hemingway's Literary Credo

In 1954, when he was awarded the Nobel Prize for Literature, Hemingway sent the following message:

> ...Things may not be immediately discernible in what a man writes, and in this sometimes he is fortunate; but eventually they are quite clear and by these and the degree of alchemy that he possesses he will endure or be forgotten.
>
> Writing, at its best, is a lonely life. Organizations for writers palliate the writer's loneliness but I doubt if they improve his writing. He grows in public stature as he sheds his loneliness and often his work deteriorates. For he does his work alone and if he is a good enough writer he must face eternity, or the lack of it each day.
>
> For a true writer each book should be a new beginning where he tries again for something that is beyond attainment. He should always try for something that has never been done or that others have tried and failed. Then, sometimes, with great luck, he will succeed.
>
> How simple the writing of literature would be if it were only necessary to write in another way what has been well written. It is because we have had such great writers in the past that a writer is driven far out past where he can go out to where no one can help him. (Baker, *The Writer As Artist*, 339)

The above passage presents Hemingway's aesthetics in a nutshell. His aesthetic opinions are stated mostly in *Death in the Afternoon*, *Green Hills of Africa* and *A Moveable Feast*. His various utterances on his art in interviews and casual conversations, his casual remarks in the course of his articles, and his introduction to *Men at War* supplement and, sometimes, only reiterate what is already stated in *Death in the Afternoon* and *Green Hills of Africa*. But, in the passage cited above, Hemingway epitomizes all his earlier pronouncements on his trade and presents his literary credo in two hundred and six words with his characteristic verbal economy.

THE AESTHETICS OF TRUTHFUL WRITING

Hemingway believes that writing at its best is a lonely life: "For he does his work alone and if he is a good enough writer, he must face eternity or the lack of it, each day." This fact underlines the need for truthfulness. Once he sheds his aesthetic loneliness and becomes part of the crowd, he will feel and write what he is supposed to feel and write. The result is insincere writing, and his work deteriorates. The writer (Hemingway speaks of writing at it best), being lonely, is answerable to himself, and any deviation from the truth would amount to self-deception. Since the writer is concerned with rendition of experience and emotion he must take care to kindle the intended emotion in the reader. This requires the writer to pinpoint the actual things which produce the emotion.

Hemingway explains it thus in *Death in the Afternoon:*

> I was trying to write then and I found the greatest difficulty, aside from knowing truly what you really felt, rather than what you were supposed to feel, and had been taught to feel, was to put down what really happened in action, what the actual things were which produced the emotion that you experienced. (10)

In his introduction to *Men at War*, Hemingway says that a writer should be of as great probity and honesty as a priest of God and is either chaste or not as a woman is either chaste or not: "A writer's job is to tell the truth. His standard of fidelity to the truth should be so high that his invention, out of his experience, should produce a truer account than anything factual can be" (XV).

Guided by this aesthetic principle of truth, he followed the kinetographic technique in the beginning, recording action like a movie-camera. His *In Our Time* vignettes are good examples of this technique. Hemingway himself makes a reference to 'cinematograph film' while describing Maera's death in the fourteenth sketch of *In Our Time*. This strengthens Earl Rovit's view that Hemingway could have been influenced by D.W. Griffith's pioneer applications of movie-camera close-ups (45).

His *In Our Time* sketches may be taken as very successful experiments in composition when he was trying hard to learn what really happened in action. It was in this period that he wrote to his father (March 20, 1925) that what he was trying to do in all of his stories was to get the feeling of actual life across—not depict it or criticize it: "only by showing both sides—putting in three dimensions, and if possible, four, could he achieve what he wanted" (Leicester Hemingway, 93). He was primarily concerned with techniques, the artist's treatment of his subject which he believed to be more important than the choice of a subject. He made this clear in his letter to his mother (February 5, 1927) defending *The Sun Also Rises* (Leicester Hemingway, 101).

One of Hemingway's strong points is his freedom from the writer's weakness of intruding upon his fictional world either to indulge in profundities himself or to make his characters do so. He keeps his eye steady on the action and emotion involved and does not allow the intellect to distract attention from them. His instinct for dramatization and his scrupulous avoidance of anything which is not absolutely necessary and irreplaceable contribute to the strength of most of his writing. Hemingway explains this point thus in *Death in the Afternoon:*

> When writing a novel, a writer should create living people; people not characters. ...If a writer can make people live there may be no great characters in his book, but it is possible that his book will remain as a whole; as an entity; as a novel. If the people the writer is making talk of old masters; of music; of modern painting; of

> letters; or of science then they should talk of those subjects in the novel. If they do not talk of those subjects and the writer makes them talk of them he is a faker, and if he talks about them himself to show how much he knows, then he is showing off. No matter how good a phrase or a simile he may have if he puts it in where it is not absolutely necessary and irreplaceable he is spoiling his work for egotism. Prose is architecture, not interior decoration, and the Baroque is over. (182)

His truthful and objective rendition of experience made him cultivate a style shorn of ornament and unnecessary detail. Even in the presentation of his aesthetic ideas he adopts an extremely simple style free from critical jargon. His work is aptly compared to the furniture that came into style at that period on the continent—"great masses of wood uncarved and unmodified by fluted pilasters and brasses and curlicues—with straight metal pipes in place of curved and claw-footed legs, and the fewest possible pieces in any one room" (J.W. Beach, 100).

Intellectual and emotional honesty should be the first guiding principle of a writer since he does his work alone and must face eternity.

THINGS NOT IMMEDIATELY DISCERNIBLE

In his acceptance message to the Swedish Academy he says: "Things may not be immediately discernible in what a man writes, ...and by these, and a degree of alchemy that he possesses, he will endure or be forgotten." Hemingway believes that if a writer knows what he is writing about and is writing truly enough, he may omit things that he knows and the reader will have a feeling of those things as strongly as though the writer had stated them. He says in *Death in the Afternoon*, "The dignity of movement of an iceberg is due to only one-eighth of it being above water" (183). Illustrating this principle to George Plimpton, Hemingway explains how he eliminated everything unnecessary to conveying the experience to the reader in *The Old Man and the Sea* which could have been over a thousand pages long:

> ...I have seen the marlin mate and know about that. So I leave that out. I've seen a school (or pod) of more than fifty sperm whales in that same stretch of water and once harpooned one nearly sixty feet in length and lost him. So I left that out. All the stories I know from the fishing village I leave out. But the knowledge is what makes the under water part of the iceberg. (Plimpton, 34-35)

This attitude reveals the influence of impressionist painters, chiefly Cezanne, on Hemingway. At the impressionist museum in Paris he showed a Cezanne to Hotchner and said that it had been his life's ambition to write "as good as that picture: Haven't made it yet, but getting closer all the time" (Hotchner, 187).

The iceberg theory operates at the different levels of depiction and dialogue. It underlines the writer's economy of expression by impression through suppression which involves suggestion and symbolism. Here Hemingway's method is very much like T. S. Eliot's "objective correlative". Like Eliot, Hemingway concentrates on the actual things which produce the emotion. Six years before Hemingway published his first important book, T. S. Eliot had published his famous essay, "Hamlet and His Problems" (1919) in which he propounded the theory of "objective correlative" which he defines as "a set of objects, a situation, a chain of events or a quotation which shall be the formula of that particular emotion" (*The Sacred Wood*, 100).

Hemingway evokes an emotional awareness in the reader by a highly selective use of suggestive pictorial detail, and has done for prose what Eliot has done for poetry. Hemingway's own observation on Eliot's theory in "Hamlet and His Problems" and his parallel passage in *Death in the Afternoon* is reported to be: "Mr. Eliot works his side of the street and I work mine" (D.S.R. Welland, 21).

It is interesting to see how Hemingway has perfected an important technique which is all right in poetry, but extremely difficult to use in prose-narrative:

> They shot the six cabinet ministers at half-past six in the morning against the wall of a hospital. There were pools of water in the courtyard. There were wet dead leaves on the paving of the courtyard. It rained hard. All the shutters of the hospital were nailed shut. One of the ministers was sick with typhoid. Two soldiers carried him down-stairs and out into the rain. They tried to hold him up against the wall but he sat down in a puddle of water. The other five stood very quietly against the wall. Finally, the officer told the soldiers it was no good trying to make him stand up. When they fired the first volley he was sitting down in the water with his head on his knees. (*In Our Time*, 63)

The writer makes no comment, expresses no emotion. It is a cool, objective recording which looks like a kinetographic reproduction of action. But the details in the picture are suggestive—the pools of water which will soon turn into pools of blood in the courtyard, the wet 'dead' leaves, the downpour which is a symbol of disaster, the shutters of the hospital, the place of healing and health, being nailed, shut, and the sick minister sitting in a puddle of water. Such emotive detail should give the reader a mental picture of the tragic scene and give him the right emotion without the writer trying to inject his emotion into the reader's mind. The cabinet ministers are killed against the wall of a hospital, and a hospital is a place where they try to prevent a man from dying. So it is appropriate that the shutters of the hospital are nailed shut, like the hospital closing its eyes to the killings. Again, the verb "nailed" evokes the image of crucifixion, which is repeated against the hospital walls. The dull, heavy word "puddle", which indicates how the sick man slumped down, is used instead of the ordinary "pool". By thus selecting and using dramatic and emotive correlatives, the writer makes the reader actively participate in the narrative.

Eliot's usual practice is to make use of complex literary symbols as objective correlatives designed to evoke a controlled emotional response, and a certain standard of literary and cultural background is necessary to appreciate these symbols in

Eliot. For example, when we read the lines "Those are pearls that were his eyes" in *The Waste Land*, we should be reminded of the same line in Ariel's song in Shakespeare's *The Tempest*, appreciate the situation of Ferdinand who thinks that he has lost his father, come back to *The Waste Land* and examine the context before we become capable of a completely satisfying response. Though Hemingway's medium is prose-narrative, which is bound to be more lucid and less abstruse and involved than poetry, he is also found to be doing certain interesting things with his images and with suggestive words under the surface of his narrative, as the following passage illustrates:

> We were in a garden in Mons. Young Buckley came in with his patrol from across the river. The first German I saw climbed up over the garden wall. We waited till he got one leg over and then potted him. He had so much equipment on and looked awfully surprised and fell down into the garden. Then three more came over further down the wall. We shot them. They all came just like that. (*In Our Time*, 33)

On the surface it is a plain narrative of how the narrator and his friends killed the attacking Germans. But the discerning reader will find the verbal trick in the use of the sharp verb of action, 'potted', with its aspirated 'p' coming abruptly after the long unit of thought "The first German I saw climbed up over the garden wall. We waited till he got one leg over and then" which suggests the difficulty the German had in climbing up the wall and the snipers' breathless waiting before potting him. The look of surprise on the face of the German with "so much equipment on" is really pathetic in that it reveals that he is not equipped with the knowledge of the ambush. All this happens in a garden. A sensitive reader who tries to read between the lines will find the garden as the objective correlative for the sin of man and the fruits thereof. The garden is the Garden of Eden from which man is expelled, and the expulsion is followed by the murder of brother by brother, which is repeated in the garden in Mons. This evokes the relevant mood and emotion. The objective correlative is not far-fetched and literary. It is a common garden even as it is a common hospital with its shutters nailed, shut and the dead leaves and puddles of water in the sketch about the shooting of the six cabinet ministers, Hemingway takes his objective correlatives from observed reality and common experience. The iceberg principle is also illustrated by the clipped dialogue with its undertones of things left unsaid, the tight-lipped conclusions of his stories, and the stoic endurance of his protagonists. The alchemy referred to in Hemingway's acceptance message consists in the writer's treatment of his subject—his technique.

TRYING FOR SOMETHING BEYOND ATTAINMENT

It is Hemingway's conviction that for a true writer each book should be a new beginning where he tries again for something that is beyond attainment. He says in *Green Hills of Africa*:

> ...a new classic does not bear any resemblance to the classics that have preceded it. It can steal from anything that it is better than, anything that is not a classic, all classics do that. Some writers are born only to help another writer to write one sentence. But it cannot derive from or resemble a previous classic. (121)

A new classic may borrow from an inferior work, but, at the same time, may not bear any resemblance either to that work or to the preceding classics, since each book is a new beginning where the writer tries for something beyond attainment, going "far out past where he can go, out to where no one can help him" like Santiago of *The Old Man and the Sea*. Every literary effort is a new challenge to a writer who wishes to last, and a real work of art lasts for ever. He says in *Green Hills of Africa*:

> A country, finally, erodes and the dust blows away, the people all die and none of them were of any importance permanently, except those who practiced arts,... A thousand years makes economics silly and a work of art endures forever, but it is very difficult to do and now it is not fashionable. (109)

Hemingway's writing has many classical virtues. His clear, objective observation of what really happens in action, stripping away what is not absolutely necessary, his concentration on the significant emotive details, his avoidance of exuberant and rhetorical writing, his habit of revising his work over and over again, and his deliberate suppression of certain details for effect point to his classical bent of mind. But the fact that his creative imagination is anchored to his own experience, making his themes highly subjective, and his belief that a new book should try for something beyond attainment mark him out as a romantic.

Hemingway believes that art is a microcosmic representation of the universe, and the important thing is to make a true work of art:

> "Let those who want to save the world if you can get to see it clear and as a whole. Then any part you make will represent the whole if it is made truly." (*Death in the Afternoon*, 261)
>
> He has chosen to work within certain limits. This has enabled him to achieve new depths in writing and explore the possibility of achieving new dimensions in prose.

5

Hemingway's Contrapuntal Theme

A close examination of Hemingway's work reveals that the whole of his *oeuvre* can be taken as a single unit the general pattern of which is implicit in his first important publication, *In Our Time,* published by William Bird's Three Mountains Press in 1924 and *In Our Time*, published by Boni and Liveright in 1925. The strange-looking title (more so on account of the small letters in the 1924 publication) is an ironic echo of "Give Peace in Our Time, O Lord" of *The Book of Common Prayer.* If there is anything conspicuous by its absence in the pages of the book, it is peace. The vignettes, between which each story is sandwiched on either side, provide a kind of background for the story besides giving a picture of the whole—a picture of violence, brutality and irrationality of our time. The short-lived happenings in the short stories are juxtaposed to the flow of life with its violence and irrationality—presenting the contrast between the two sets of time.

This theme is made explicit in the ironic juxtaposition between the two epigraphs prefacing his next important work, *The Sun Also Rises:*

> "You are all a lost generation."—Gertrude Stein in conversation
>
> "One generation passeth away, and another generation cometh: but the earth abideth forever...."—Ecclesiastes

Hemingway seems to be thinking of the pageant of passing generations against the vast background of the everlasting earth, illustrating the dialectic between horological time and geological time, between the ephemeral and the continual. He finds an objective correlative for this juxtaposition nine years later in the Gulf stream which "has moved, as it moves, since before man" with the flotsam of palm-fronds, corks, bottles, used electric light globes and other things:

> ... and the palm-fronds of our victories, the worn light bulbs of our discoveries and the empty condoms of our great loves float with no significance against one single, lasting thing, the stream. (*Green Hills of Africa*, 148-150)

The Gulf Stream is the correlative image for the flux of life and the eternal earth. Counterpointed by it are a variety of human activities which have absolutely no effect on it. It goes on undisturbed around the little human drama on which interest is focused and which is like a drama or a movie in a theatre which has little effect on the life that flows outside.

The awareness of the futility of all human endeavour is like a shadow of the original chaos on the human mind: Hemingway calls it *nada* and makes it the subject of his story, "A Clean Well-Lighted Place". Night and death are its external and concrete symbols in the physical world. *Nada*, night and death figure prominently in most of Hemingway's work.

In man, a clean well-lighted place is a stout heart, which involves the courage to fight the good fight, the endurance to suffer pain without complaint, and the adherence to a certain code of conduct. It leads to victory in the face of defeat, converting material defeat into moral or spiritual triumph. It is illustrated by Manuel Garcia, the forgotten old bullfighter, in "Undefeated", by Jesus in "Today Is Friday", by Robert Jordan in *For Whom the Bell Tolls,* and by Santiago in *The Old Man and the Sea.*

Hemingway's emphasis on courage, according to Cleanth Brooks, is significant and, perhaps, necessary as a first step in moving back towards the Christian virtues: "Hemingway, of course, stops short of the domain of Christianity proper, but he does see that the man who lacks courage, a mere slave to his fears, is not truly free and not truly human" (15). Courage has a vital relevance to our situation. E.M. Halliday puts it thus:

> In the image of the crucifixion, which has haunted Hemingway from "Today Is Friday"(1929) to *The Old Man and the Sea*, it is the unique courage of the forsaken and crucified man—God that takes his attention. ...we are part of a universe offering no assurance beyond the grave, and we are to make what we can of life by a pragmatic ethic spun bravely out of man himself in full and steady cognizance that the end is darkness. (299)

Courage, endurance and acting one's part honestly and well even against heavy odds offer the only hope, according to Hemingway, against the enveloping *nada*.

That courage is central to Hemingway's attitude to life is clear from the following extract from his introduction to *Men at War*, which shows that, both as writer and man, he valued it very highly:

> I was very ignorant at nineteen and had read little and I remember the sudden happiness and the feeling of having a permanent protecting talisman when a young British Officer I met in the hospital first wrote out for me, so that I could remember them, these lines:
>
> "By my troth, I care not; a man can die but once: we owe God a death...and let it go which way it will, he that dies this year is quit for the next."
>
> That is probably the best thing that is written in this book and, with nothing else, a man can get along all right on that. (xiv)

Hemingway shows us the growth of a young boy called Nick Adams through violence, suffering and love in *In Our Time*. Nick reappears again and again in *Men without Women* and *Winner Take Nothing*.

THE EVOLUTION OF THE HERO

The story of Nick follows the same pattern as the age-old mythical hero's, outlined by Joseph Campbell, involving separation, initiation and return (30), but with an important difference. While the mythical hero gains extraordinary knowledge and power and returns with the power to bestow boons or with a great message, Nick returns with only the scars, both physical and psychic, sustained during his adventures. He returns, not to heal and help others but to recuperate his physical and mental health. The injury Nick suffers in Chapter VI of *In Our Time* has a special significance, for it is not only based on Hemingway's own experience but becomes a recurring theme in Hemingway's works. All his heroes are wounded, in some degree or other, at some point in their lives, like Jake of *The Sun Also Rises*, Frederic Henry of *A Farewell to Arms*, Harry Morgan of *To Have and Have Not,* Robert Jordan of *For Whom the Bell Tolls,* Col. Cantwell of *Across the River and into the Trees*, and Santiago of *The Old Man and the Sea*. The protagonist demonstrates a superior love illustrating the definition of love given by the priest in *A Farewell to Arms*: "when you love, you wish to do things for. You wish to sacrifice for. You wish to serve" (75).

Hemingway seems to say that this is all man can do, caught up as he is in a pageant of passing generations, violence and conflict. Self-control and efficiency in whatever one does, courage, love and endurance—these virtues make a clean well-lighted place, which can keep off *nada.* He is keenly aware of the ironic juxtaposition between the lost generation and the abiding earth. He seems to say that all generations are lost against the abiding earth just as "the palm-fronds of our victories, the worn light bulbs of our discoveries and the empty condoms of our great loves" are lost against the great Gulf Stream.

This contrapuntal theme operates at two levels in Hemingway's work. At one level it is expressed by the conflict between dark forces like *nada*, night and death on the one hand and the bright forces like courage, love, a self-imposed discipline and code of conduct which go into the making of a clean well-lighted place, which can resist the gloom. This falls into the pattern of the traditional Manichean conflict between good and evil. At another, slightly higher level, is the Ecclesiastesian theme of the anti-thesis between the ephemeral generations and the everlasting earth, of the futility of all human endeavour against the "one single lasting thing—the stream".

Apart from the evolution of the hero following the mythical pattern of Separation, Initiation, Fabulous Achievements and Return, there is a different kind of evolution of a mundane modern nature from young Nick to old Santiago tracing the growth of a young man through varied experiences, trials and tribulations from novel to novel, marking the changes, both physical and psychological, in his nature. The ambience, through which the protagonist travels through novel after novel, is one of violence and brutality. It is interesting to trace briefly the evolution of these narratives with their themes, techniques and protagonists.

IN OUR TIME

Hemingway explains the plan of his *In Our Time* thus in a letter to Edmund Wilson (October 18, 1924), quoted by the latter in his "Emergence of Ernest Hemingway" (*Hemingway and His Critics: An International Anthology*):

> Finished the book of 14 stories with a chapter of *In our Time* between each story—that is the way they were meant to go—to give the picture of the whole between examining it in detail. Like looking with your eyes at something, say a passing coastline, and then looking at it with 15x binoculars or rather, may be, looking at it and then going in and living in it— and then coming out and looking it again. (60)

The vignettes which escort each story on either side of it provide a kind of background for the story besides giving a picture of the whole, a picture of the violence, brutality and irrationality of our time. The good things of life which make it enjoyable are somehow inextricably related to its tragic violence, and this makes the irony of life all the more poignant.

Edmund Wilson sees this ironic bond between the joy and brutality of life which characterizes *In our Time*:

> Life is fine; the woods are enjoyable; fishing is enjoyable; being with one's friends is enjoyable; even the war is enjoyable. But the brutality is always there,... through all Nick's tranquil exhilaration we are made conscious in a

> curious way of the cruelty involved for the fish—...The condition of life is still pain—and every calm or contented surface still vibrates with its pangs. The resolution of that discord in art makes the beauty of Hemingway's stories. (Introd. xi)

The vignettes and stories work together in giving a thematic unity to the book. There is also a perfect unity of actions in the stories, which deal with the growth of Nicholas Adams into Jake Barnes, Frederic Henry, Harry Morgan, Robert Jordan, Col. Cantwell, and Santiago, heroes of the novels of his lifetime as well as Thomas Hudson and David Bourne, protagonists of the posthumous novels. *In our Time*, though a collection of stories, is not like his other story collections, and has a structure of all its own. It cannot be treated as a novel either, since its stories are independent units with a thread of continuity running through most of them.

The lake at the commencement of the book (*Indian Camp*) becomes the "Big Two-Hearted River" at the end with its dark dangerous swamp in which Nick is afraid to fish. Like the Gulf Stream, it stands for the flux of life, which serves as a background for the human drama dealing with the ineffectuality of the doctors, the battlers, the soldiers, the Elliots, and men and women in general. The interest is focused on this drama. As the focus is lifted at the end of the last story, and as Nick, on his way back to his camp, looks back, the river is seen through the trees. *In Our Time* shows the growth of the Hemingway hero from a young boy (Nick) into a man of the world, committed to the woman he deeply loves (Jake and Frederick Henry) and an amoral man of action who believes in himself and his lone effort (Henry Morgan), and a brave soldier who stakes his life for a cause (Robert Jordan), a World War II veteran, who visits the city he loves best for the last time (Col. Cantwell), and an old fisherman, who catches the biggest ever marlin of his life and fights hordes of sharks in the Gulf Stream (Santiago).

Nick's consciousness represents the author's credo of unblinking, unflinching, and accurate reporting. He is, in the words of Tony Tanner, "the ideal Hemingway 'eye'":

> What Hemingway makes use of is Nick's 'first chastity of mind' which wonderingly notes the details without being tempted away into the blurring habits of theorizing. If there is a symbolic 'first man in the world' hidden inside the name of Adams it is only because Nick retains that essential integrity of the senses even when confronted with the most brutal disillusioning scenes." (242)

If young Nick *wonderingly* notes his experiences, old mature Santiago *lovingly* notes them. Adam, the generic man who wonders at what he sees and goes through, grows into Saint James, whose love encompasses "both man and bird and beast". Nick is the first in a long line of Hemingway's fictional selves.

THE SUN ALSO RISES

The Sun Also Rises is a good example of how fiction can be at once simple and complex. Deriving from Hemingway's own experiences at the Pamplona fiesta, this novel is based on fact for the most part providing Hemingway with the opportunity of writing about "what really happened in action" and the things that actually produced the emotion. The bars, the drunkenness, the small talk, the promiscuity, and the apparent aimlessness of the characters bespeak the sad effect of the war on a generation and create an atmosphere for the action to take place in. The narrator-protagonist, Jake, is the worst affected by the war, being emasculated by a wound. His hopeless love for Brett, a nymphomaniac, who is also madly in love with him but has to find satisfaction in other men's arms, forms the central ironic theme of the story which multiplies itself into different ironical situations. Cohn loves Brett, but Brett is engaged to Mike not because she loves him but because he is her sort; she takes a momentary fancy to Romero, the bullfighter, but decides later not to ruin him. There is irony in the fact that, while the characters drink, dance and make merry, and are happy to all appearances, they are extremely unhappy in their hearts for some reason or other. Jake expresses this irony when he says: "It is awfully easy to be hard-boiled about everything in the daytime, but at night it is another thing" (35).

between wounded Nick and the Red Cross nurse, Luz, is presented. Luz is Catherine's counterpart in the story. Nick is forsaken by Luz who breaks off her engagement in a letter. But in the novel Catherine dies in childbirth at the end. In both cases a farewell to the arms of love is indicated along with a farewell to the arms of war.

When the different strands which go into the making of the novel are taken into consideration, a complex pattern emerges with love, war and death as the major themes. According to Philip Young, the courses of love and war in the novel run exactly parallel so that in the end we feel we have read one story, not two. In his affair with the war, Henry goes through six phases: desultory participation, serious action, wound, recuperation in Milan, and retreat leading to desertion. His relationship with Catherine undergoes six precisely corresponding stages: trifling sexual affair, actual love, conception, confinement in the Alps, trip to the hospital and death (*Reconsideration*, 93).

In both the courses of love and war, the protagonist progresses from a casual pleasure-loving attitude to a serious, responsible view of things and a sober understanding of things.

In both the early novels, as in the collection of stories, *In Our Time*, the protagonists make a separate peace. Nick and Rinaldi make a separate peace in Chapter VI. In *The Sun also Rises*, Jake and Brett make a separate peace even as they become mature and responsible in the end. *In a Farewell to Arms*, Frederick Henry and Catherine make a separate peace when they realize the meaning of true love as defined by the priest. But Nick, Jake, and Frederick Henry do not realize the value of social obligations and commitments. They do not know the importance of fighting for a cause or loving their fellow-creatures. They share the wound which is common to the protagonists of all the novels, and which is a projection of Hemingway's own wound in Italy. They adhere to a code, which has become famous as the Hemingway Code which consists of the courage to fight the good fight, the endurance to suffer pain without complaint, and the adherence to a certain code of conduct.

Nick's surname suggests Adam, an *Old Testament* name standing for the first man or the generic man, and Hemingway's narrative starts with Adam's initiation into a knowledge of birth and death and, later, his fall from the freight-train when he is thrown out by the brakeman. Adam yields place to Jacob in *The Sun Also Rises*. As Jacob wrestled with God "until the breaking of the day" (Genesis, 32: 24-30), Jake Barnes wrestles with his own consciousness all the night. It is difficult to say whether he received a blessing in the end like Jacob. If a thorough disillusionment resulting in the ultimate wisdom in humility is a blessing, Jake receives it at the end in the usual ironic mode characteristic of Hemingway. This kind of wisdom in humility dawns on other Hemingway heroes like Frederick Henry, Harry Morgan, Robert Jordan, Col. Cantwell and Santiago in the end. Once we start looking at the suggestive titles and proper nouns, Jake Barnes fits in beautifully with the pattern for it is Jacob with a difference—a barren Jacob. Look at what God said to the Biblical Jacob blessing him:

> And God appeared unto Jacob again, when he came out of Padanaram, and blessed him.
>
> And God said unto him, thy name is Jacob: thy name shall not be called any more Jacob, but Israel shall be thy name: and he called his name Israel.
>
> And God said unto him, I am God Almighty: be fruitful and multiply: a nation and a company of nations shall be of thee, and kings shall come out of thy loins;
>
> And the land which I gave Abraham and Isaac, to thee will I give it, and to thy seed after thee will I give the land. (Genesis, 35:9-12)

Jacob Barnes presents a glaring contrast to the Biblical Jacob in that the former was emasculated by a war wound and therefore barren, while the latter became fruitful and multiplied, and his seed inherited the land. Jacob Barnes is like the barren Fisher King of the myths, who belonged to the "lost generation" in a war-torn wasteland.

The remedy for this barrenness, the cure for this wasteland and the redemption of this "lost generation" can be found in a

TO HAVE AND HAVE NOT

This novel is in three parts—"Spring", "Autumn", and "Winter". Part one, entitled "Spring" is told by Harry Morgan, the protagonist. It shows how Harry, who had the honesty and fear of law to turn down an offer of three thousand dollars to smuggle four men from Cuba to the U.S.A., becomes a man-runner and a crooked murderer when he is cheated by a wealthy man who has chartered his boat and lost his fishing tackle. The social theme of how an honest have-not is corrupted and changed into a criminal by the haves is presented in the first part which, ironically, is the 'spring' in the life of a criminal created by society.

The first-person narration gives us an immediacy of experience and contributes to the compactness of narrative in the manner of the two early novels. But, as we go through the novel and find that Harry dies before the end of the novel, we begin to wonder how and at what point he tells the story. This is one of the most serious problems the first-person method can give rise to.

Therefore, Hemingway employs the third-person point of view in part Two of the novel, "Autumn". In this part, we find Harry turning a rum-runner and losing an arm in the process. It is clear that he will lose his boat also. He has become a hardened criminal now and this part is the autumn—"the season of mellow fruitfulness"—in a criminal's life. Thus the title "Autumn" is itself ironic. This irony is underlined by the fact that Harry was a member of the police force up in Miami, and by nemesis overtaking the criminal in "Autumn" for the crime committed in "Spring". Harry broke Mr. Sing's arm before killing him and has already started paying for it by losing his arm, and we know that he had only the final instalment to pay—arm for arm, and life for life.

The third part entitled "Winter" describes a criminal's end, the winter of a criminal's life. Harry agrees to smuggle four Cubans across the Gulf Stream not knowing that they are trigger happy bank-robbers and revolutionaries. He kills all four of them and is fatally wounded in the fight.

The novel thus describes the growth and death of a criminal made by a corrupt society and, throughout, the corrupting influence of big money is felt. The paradox of the Haves being Have-Nots in regard to manliness and morality as contrasted with the Have-Not, Morgan, who is rich in those qualities though forced by circumstances to do illegal things is developed in the third part by alternating Morgan's story with the Gordons' and other Haves'. The domestic felicity of the Morgans' is set off by the nasty mess of the Gordons, the Bradleys and the Hollises have made of their marriages.

Harry, the protagonist, is presented at the end as learning a truth and struggling hard to express it before his death: "No matter how a man alone ain't got no bloody chance." This realization that a man should team up with others for any effective action dawns on the Hemingway hero at the end of Hemingway's third novel. After this, the Hemingway hero does not crave for a separate peace, and pursues a social cause/ course with a sense of commitment, flowing out with love and fellow-feeling for one and all.

When we find Santiago struggling alone against the marlin and, later, fighting the sharks, we hark back to the last words of Harry Morgan. The connection between the two is further emphasized by the marlin which he and Johnson try to catch unsuccessfully. This marlin may be interpreted as a symbol for the big prize Hemingway was already aspiring for at that time after three tremendously successful works of fiction.

FOR WHOM THE BELL TOLLS

Based on the Spanish civil war and Hemingway's knowledge of Spain and its people and his commitment to the Republican cause, this novel has the same structure as *A Farewell to Arms* in that there is a parallel movement of the themes of war and love here. The war theme centres round Robert Jordan, the bridge-blower, and the guerillas he works with, for by now the Hemingway hero has learnt that 'separate peace' does not serve any useful purpose and that he should work with others for a cause.

Thematically, the novel arises in part from the last words of Harry Morgan that "a man alone ain't got no bloody chance." But there is a subtle difference in the levels of thinking between Harry's last words which emphasize collective action or the futility of individual action and the Donnean theme of the oneness of mankind which is used as an epigraph for the novel:

> No man is an *island*, intire of itself; every man is a peace of the *continent*, a part of the maine; if a *clod* bee washed away by the *sea*, *Europe* is the lesse, as well as if a *Promontorie* were, as well as if a Mannor of thy *friends* or of thine owne were; any man's death diminishes *me*, because I am involved in Mankinde; And therefore never send to know for whom the *bell* tolls; it tolls for *thee*.

This is related to the war-and-death-theme; and the love-theme as it is developed in the novel is also related to the Donnean conception with its reference to the "Phoenix riddle" ("The Canonization") and of the lover and the beloved being one:

> Our two soules, therefore, which are one,
> Though I must goe, endure not yet
> A breach, but an expansion,
> Like Gold to ayery thinnesse beate
> ("A Valediction Forbidding Mourning")

Jake of *The Sun also Rises* thinks it his responsibility to help Brett whatever the circumstances may be. All that he wants is to make a separate peace with her in spite of his own personal sorrow. Frederick Henry of *A Farewell to Arms* learns the essence of love from his friend and mentor—the priest, who serves as the code hero who teaches the hero: "When you love you wish to do things for; you wish to sacrifice for; you wish to serve." His attitude changes but still he cannot translate theory into practice which Catherine does. Harry Morgan of *To Have and Have Not* acts the part of the ideal husband without knowing the theory and is far too busy in his criminal activities to think of love and its significance.

But Robert Jordan demonstrates the priest's theory of love in action and fulfills the role of the ideal lover, who does things for his beloved, serves her and sacrifices his life for her. The paradox of the lover and the loved being one, is at the centre of the novel like the bridge which joins the two sides of a gorge and makes them one. Robert Jordan and Maria are one, but when wounded Jordan tells Maria to go away with Pablo's band, Maria is both of them: "The me in thee. Now you go for us both. Truly. We both go in thee now" (464). Robert W. Lewis, Jr. puts it in the form of a convenient equation when he says that one plus one equals one, but when eros combines with agape, one minus one also equals one (170).

The Hemingway hero's baptism through rain, which is a predominant symbol in *A Farewell to Arms*, and which is heightened by his plunge into the Tagliamento and his final walk back in the rain to his hotel, leads us to the Jordan. Robert Jordan, whose surname suggests the river that baptized Jesus Christ, stands prominently between Jake and Santiago, like the baptized river which transformed Israel (Jacob) into the apostle, St. James. The kind of love expounded by the priest in *A Farewell to Arms* begins to bloom in *For Whom the Bell Tolls*. It does not appear to be by mere accident that rain does not figure in the last three novels. Its purpose served as an instrument of baptism, rain is no longer needed, and the Christological figure peeps out occasionally through Cantwell and frequently through Santiago who, at the end, becomes identified with it.

Interior monologues are used to a much greater advantage in this novel than in Hemingway's earlier fiction. They not only present the characters' thought-processes and throw light on his character, memories and dreams but reveal some of the basic ironic patterns reflecting the vanity of human plans and efforts. Robert Jordan's belief that "the bridge can be the point on which the future of the human race can turn" (43) is finally reduced to total insignificance in the context of the war, and all the efforts and sacrifices in blowing it are wasted. Robert Jordan's interior monologues help in bringing out the tragedy of the story—a tragedy of which he seems to be aware throughout. It is a tragedy of action unlike the first two novels which are tragedies of helplessness. Right from the beginning Jordan has his fears that the attack is doomed to failure, being aware of the composition of the Republican leadership. But he is a disciplined soldier and his business is to carry out his orders:

> Neither you nor this old man is anything. You are instruments to do your duty. There are necessary orders that are no fault of yours and there is a bridge and that bridge can be the point on which the future of the human race can turn. As it can turn on everything that happens in this war. (43)

The tragedy is Jordan's personal tragedy at the primary level, and involves Golz's attack and the Spanish civil war at the secondary level. The dramatic focus in the novel is on Golz's attack in general and Jordan's involvement with the bridge, with the guerillas, and with Maria in particular. Whatever may be said about the Spanish civil war in general is only incidental and is of background importance only. Pilar's account of the Republican brutality and Maria's account of the Falangist brutality are couched in flashback narration as unpleasant memories and do not form part of the onward-moving narrative. Robert Jordan's interior monologues are purposeful and contribute to the total effect. Even his memories of the Gay-lord's and Karkov, besides giving us an idea of the international complexion of the civil war, show the importance of people like Karkov which has a special significance in the context of Andres' mission. Several chapters later, Karkov helps Andres overcome the frustrating obstacles put in his way by Andre Massart.

The protagonist's mind is given a great deal of importance in this novel, and a sizable slice of the novel concerns his reflections. W.M. Frohock, in *The Novel of Violence in America*, observes:

> And at the end, his understanding of the story becomes one with the reader's, so that the tragic irony—the

> discrepancy between the hero's understanding of his misfortune and the audience's misunderstanding of it—is resolved. The reader has no trouble in identifying himself satisfactorily with Jordan through their common humanity; he admits that, in true fact, this man's death diminishes him; pity and terror are legitimatized. (189-190)

The Hemingway hero who, as Nick Adams, Jake Barnes and Frederick Henry, sought separate peace in a narrow-minded selfish way, realized his mistake as Harry Morgan, and has now matured enough to feel that he is involved in mankind and that everyman's death diminishes him. This leads to a greater and better understanding of life and wider love for his fellow men as Col. Cantwell, and eventually extends to birds and beasts as Santiago.

ACROSS THE RIVER AND INTO THE TREES

The subject of this novel is Colonel Cantwell's last visit to Venice, the city he loves most, and his preparedness for death, which comes at the end of his visit. He visits Venice for the duck-shoot and for a meeting with Countess Renata, his nineteen-year-old beloved, and his old friends. The duration of the visit is two days, or to be exact, less than two days for, at the end, the early darkness of the second day begins. But when we include the Colonel's medical examination, the time of action will be three days. It starts with the Colonel giving death and ends with his taking death. There is an attempt at observing the three classical unities in a greater measure than in *For Whom the Bell Tolls*. The new technique of alternating memory with actual experience, shifting of point of view, flashback, and interior monologue, which have been used since the great stories, "The Snows of Kilimanjaro" and "The Short Happy Life of Francis Macomber", the experimental novel, *To Have and Have Not*, and *For Whom the Bell Tolls* are used in this novel too.

Colonel Cantwell, the protagonist, is about the same age as Hemingway was when he wrote this novel. Hemingway loved Venice and the beautiful Adriana Ivancich, who inspired the creation of the character of Renata, who was a sort of Venus, the presiding deity of Venice (Venizia). The actual experience, in the flashback narration, is the Colonel's visit to Venice and his meeting with his beloved Renata. The memories deal with his experiences in the Second World War—"the sad science" of soldiering. He feels better, "purging" his bitterness as he tells Renata about the war, which marks a great improvement, in moral terms, on Robert Jordan's character. Throughout, he makes a conscious effort to get the better of his temper, to be understanding and sympathetic, forgiving, and kind. He tries to convert his disappointment into a positive effort to satisfy and please Renata. They both know that the Colonel's end is near and their last meeting, while it brings a serious disappointment, reveals the selfless love of the Colonel who finds his pleasure only in giving it to Renata. But the alternation of memory with actual experience, which contributes to the power of narration lends the right perspective to the reader.

Philip Young, referring to the view that the marlin of *The Old Man and the Sea* is *Across the River and into the Trees,* which was torn to pieces by reviewers and critics, and Hemingway's own description of it as his calculus, comments thus:

> It is not safe to dismiss such a statement as simply pretentious. Years before, when he wrote of the 'fourth and fifth dimension that can be gotten' in prose it turned out that he had something in mind. Perhaps some day it can be shown how the calculus, which is often described as a symbolic means of "grasping the fleeting instant", throws a more attractive light on the novel than has yet been observed. (*Reconsideration*, 275)

Across the River and into the Trees demonstrates an obvious attempt at grasping the fleeting instant. The novel is, in a way, an enlargement of the Colonel's fleeting impression of his two-day visit to Venice in the midst of his duck-shoot. The author, who is conscious of his *Othello* parallel, might have in mind the fleeting instant before Othello's death when his memory recaptures for a moment all the romance and tragedy of his life.

> Then must you speak
> Of one that lov'd not wisely, but too well;
> . . . .
> And say besides, that in Aleppo once,
> Where a malignant and turban'd Turk
> Beat a Venetian and traduc'd the state,
> I took by the throat the circumcised dog,
> And smote him—thus.
>
> (Act V, sc ii, ll. 346-59)

Across the River and into the Trees is an attempt at catching hold of such a fleeting instant before the Colonel's death and working back towards a narrative pattern involving the preceding two days. The ambitious symbolic construct, verging on the allegorical, which he builds upon the narrative with Dantesque overtones and Christological references, adds a new dimension to the novel and its hero.

The image of Charon rowing souls across the Acheron, which appears in "Indian camp" as the Indian rowing Nick and his father, and, at the end of the story, as his father rowing the boat in which Nick sits, recurs again in a more prominent and meaningful way in *Across the River and into the Trees*. The novel follows the pattern of Dante's *The Divine Comedy* at the symbolic level with many structural variations. The Charon-figure is there rowing the Colonel's boat in the dark of the early morning at the commencement of the novel. But Jackson, the driver, plays Dante to the Colonel, who, like Virgil, shows and explains to him the important spots of Venice. After meeting Renata, his Beatrice, he is completely involved with her, and Jackson keeps in the background for the most part until the Colonel emerges out of Paradise. Again we have the Charon-and-Acheron image, and, towards the end, Jackson-Virgil takes over the job of guiding the Colonel out of Venice. There is a reversal of roles again in the relationship between Colonel-Dante and Renata-Beatrice, with the Colonel acting as guide to Renata and enlightening her about the war. Venice stands for the entire world of *The Divine Comedy* with its infernal and purgatorial horrors transformed into the Colonel's memories of the war and its heavens shrunk into the aura around Renata.

Hemingway provides us with a clue to this Dantesque parallelism in the following conversation in *Across the River and into the Trees:*

> "You sound like Dante", she said sleepily.
> "I am Mister Dante", he said.
> "For the moment."
> And for a while he was and he drew all the circles. They were as unjust as Dante's but he drew them. (246)

Dante's prayer to Mary towards the end when he meets St. Bernard has its parallel in the Colonel's reflection that he may get Christian towards the end:

> You going to run as a Christian? You might give it an honest try. She would like you better that way. Or would like you better that way. Or would she? I don't know, he said frankly. I honest to Christ don't know.
> Maybe I will get Christian toward the end. Yes, he said, maybe you will. Who wants to make a bet on that? (291)

The novel has also a Biblical hue. The Colonel's last three days are packed with love and forgiveness—love for Venice, for Renata, for Gran Maestro, and for everybody he meets and everything he touches, and forgiveness of the boatman who offends him. He finds fault with himself when he speaks badly of people (229), and makes a conscious effort, not to be bitter about things (252). His bad hand which Renata loves much and which he uses to satisfy her while foregoing his own erotic fulfillment, is like the nailed hand of Jesus.

The title derives from Stonewall Jackson's words before his death and sounds slightly ironical as the Colonel, who does everything "carefully and well" repeats the words, "Let us cross over the river and rest under the shade of the trees" (307), to the General's namesake, driver Jackson, and finally dies in his car. He shares the General's ill-health and badly injured right hand, and qualities of head and heart.

An important feature of the novel is the narrative focus, which is on the Colonel from beginning to end. It is not shifted even for a moment. This is an important shift in technique from *For Whom the Bell Tolls*, where it is shifted from Jordan and the bridge, to Pilar and her story, Maria and her story, Andrés and his adventures, Golz and his predicament, and other situations. The narrative situation is reduced to the simplest terms, and the protagonist is the only character who counts and his mind briefly becomes the scene of a dialectic between fun and love (71). This dialectic is taken up two hundred pages later when the Colonel reveals the Supreme Secret of the Mysterious Order to Renata: "Love is love and fun is fun. But it is always so quiet when the gold fish die" (271). The Colonel, who is the Supreme Commander of the order, has had his share of fun as seen in his activities in Venice including the duck-shoot and learnt his lesson in love as revealed in his relations with Renata, and what remains now is that he should die a quiet and graceful death. This technique of uninterrupted and undeviating focus on a single character enhances the image of the hero and is exploited to the best advantage in Hemingway's next novel, *The Old Man and the Sea*.

The Colonel's forgiveness of the boatman even before learning of his "over-liberation" by the allies, which forms part of the main action of the story, points to the central paradox of the Colonel's sexual disappointment resulting in a triumph of love and compassion. At one level the Colonel fails to find fulfillment in his life. Renata disappoints him in a way; and his duck-shoot is spoiled by the boatman. But at another, more important because subjective level he has no regrets at the time of death. In fact, his feeling is one of fulfillment: "I've always been a lucky son of a bitch" (307).

The Hemingway hero, Nick, of *In Our Time* becomes a soldier in *The Sun Also Rises* and a lieutenant in *A Farewell to Arms*, an ex-member of the Police Force in *To Have and Have Not*, and then becomes an expert dynamiter and bridge-blower with considerable experience in *For Whom the Bell Tolls* and then rises to the position of a Colonel in *Across the River and into the Trees*, before becoming the wise old Santiago whose love extends beyond Venice and its people to the vast sea and its birds and beasts, not to speak of the people around him.

THE OLD MAN AND THE SEA

The Hemingway hero crosses a river as the boy, Nick Adams, under the protective care of his father in *In our Time*. Later he fishes in the "Big Two-Hearted River" while recuperating from his traumatic shock in war. In *The Sun Also Rises*, he relaxes fishing at Burguet. In *A Farewell to Arms*, he jumps into the Tagliamento and escapes from the military police. In *To Have and Have Not*, he smuggles guns and men across the Gulf Stream. In *For Whom the Bell Tolls*, he blows a bridge across the river. In *Across the River and into the Trees,* he floats on the water ways of Venice in the company of his beloved Renata distributing love and forgiveness to one and all. In *The Old Man and the Sea*, he rows a skiff on the vast sea struggling against a huge marlin and, after vanquishing it, fighting off the predatory sharks, risking his life in the process. His boat is so small on the limitless expanse of water that the planes searching for him cannot find his boat. The insignificance of man *vis-à-vis* the vastness and power of the sea and the earth are brought into focus here. This makes us hark back to the memorable description of the Gulf Stream in *Green Hills of Africa*.

> ...and the palm-fronds of our victories, the worn light bulbs of our discoveries, and the empty condoms of our great loves float with no significance against one single, lasting thing—the stream. (148-150)

In all the preceding novels, Hemingway's contrapuntal theme is implied and suggested, but in *The Old Man and the Sea* it becomes explicit and dramatic and this is expressed by the title itself. In the process, we see the growth of the hero from young Nick Adams to the wise old Santiago passing through various experiences until, in the end, he not only faces the sea but passes through the problems and obstacles it places in his way and catches the biggest ever fish of his life and defends it against the bloodthirsty sharks demonstrating the indefatigable and unconquerable spirit of man coupled with the humility and love of a wise man of a noble spirit.

6

A Brief Summary of *The Old Man and the Sea*

The Old Man and the Sea is the story of an old Cuban fisherman's struggles to catch a great fish. He has a devoted companion—a young boy, who has no part in the old man's struggles.

The novel is based on the real life story of an old Cuban fisherman catching a great fish and losing it to the sharks. Hemingway writes about it in a letter published in *Esquire* (April 1936), fifteen years before the publication of the novelette, under the caption "On the Blue Water : A Gulf Stream Letter":

> Another time an old man fishing alone in a skiff out of cabanas hooked a great marlin that, on the heavy sash cord hard-line, pulled the skiff far out to sea. Two days later the old man was picked up by fishermen sixty miles to the eastward, the head and forward part of the marlin lashed alongside. What was left of the fish, less than half, weighed eight hundred pounds. The old man had stayed with him a day, a night, a day and another night while the fish swam deep and pulled the boat upon him and harpooned him. Lashed alongside the sharks had hit him and the old man had fought them out alone in the Gulf Stream in a skiff, clubbing them, stabbing at them, lunging at them with an oar until he was exhausted and the sharks had eaten all that they could hold. He was crying in the boat when the fishermen picked him up,

half crazy from his loss, and the sharks were circling the boat (William White, 239-40).

This real life incident inspires Hemingway first to write a brief account in *Esquire* magazine and, fifteen years later, to write a great short novel. There are two characters in the opening part of the novel—an old fisherman and his boy-companion, and only one character—the old fisherman in most of the novel, and some tourists and, later, the old fisherman and his boy-companion in the last part.

Santiago is a seventy-year old fisherman, who lives in Havana, Cuba. He fishes the Gulf Stream for eighty-four days without catching a fish. The boy, Manolin, who loves Santiago and looks after him, accompanies him for the first forty days, but now his parents conclude that the old man is hopelessly unlucky and sends him on another boat. Still Manolin serves the old man bringing him food and beer and helps him carry his tackle to the boat. They discuss baseball in the old man's shack. The old man sleeps alone dreaming of his youth in Africa and lions on the beach.

Santiago is not interested in catching small fish; he wants to catch the biggest fish ever caught in the Gulf Stream. He thinks of the sea as a woman. On the eighty-fifth day, he sets sail again determined to catch the biggest ever fish far out in the sea. He sails far out, sets his lines and waits for the big fish. He watches a school of dolphins pursue flying fish and curses a Portuguese man-of-war that drifts nearby. He catches a small tuna and waits for the big fish. When it comes, it pulls at the bait gently. The veteran fisherman learns later that it is a marlin nibbling his bait six hundred feet below. He senses the right moment and pulls hard and the long struggle begins.

It is now noon and the sun grows hot. Santiago feeds the marlin some more line as the fish swims away towing the skiff north-westwards. Santiago waits for the marlin to get tired. He holds the heavy line in his calloused hands and carries it across his shoulders. The fish drags the boat after him all afternoon and into the evening and night. Santiago wishes he had the boy with him. The old man feels that his endurance is under pressure but he is determined to subdue his adversary alone. He thinks about the fish at the end of the line and about other great fish he has caught. The fish is strong and, during the night, he lurches, and Santiago falls down on his face. His cheek is cut, but he does not relax his hold on the line.

Next morning the old man is stiff and hungry. But he does not pull the line tight lest the fish should break it. The birds appear above and Santiago talks to them. All of a sudden the fish surges and the line cuts through his hand. His hand hurts but the thought that the fish is getting tired gives him pleasure. He wonders what the fish plans. He thinks that the fish is his brother but he must be stronger to overcome his prey. He suffers a cramp in his left hand and worries about it.

The line suddenly becomes slack and the fish leaps out making an arc above the surface of the water. It is the largest marlin Santiago has ever seen, longer than his skiff. Santiago prays for victory and wants to show the fish "what a man can do and what a man endures". The fish tows the skiff eastwards all afternoon and into the night. Santiago tries to gain strength from the memory of a hand-game he won several years ago at a tavern. He tries to draw strength from the thought of the boy and the baseball Champion, DiMaggio. He catches a dolphin and eats it to satisfy his hunger and gain strength. The marlin jumps again in the night causing another cut in Santiago's hands. He dozes in the middle of the struggle and dreams of Africa and the lions.

On the morning of the third day the fish leaps up again and again, and the line lacerates Santiago's hands. He begins to shorten the line and every time it tears his hands causing him excruciating pain. He washes his bleeding hands in the sea and resumes drawing in the line while the tiring marlin moves round the skiff in ever-narrowing concentric circles. Just before the fish comes close enough for the old man's harpoon he begs it not to kill them both. He is filled with love and admiration for the fish and exclaims that he does not care if the noble creature, who is at once his brother and enemy, kills him. It matters little who kills whom. Finally, Santiago harpoons and kills the mighty marlin and lashes it to the side of his skiff.

An hour later, his nightmare begins. A Mako shark attacks the dead marlin and takes away a slice of its flesh. Then come the galanos in large numbers. Santiago fights them off with all his might, not only defending his victory but the dignity of the dead fish. In spite of his brave fight, the sharks mutilate the fish. He wonders whether he has committed a sin in killing the fish, but realizes that a man may be destroyed but not defeated. Santiago is very sorry that the fish, his brother, is dead. He knows that he is fighting a losing battle but doggedly fights on. He fights the sharks desperately in the dark, losing his knife and club and breaking his tiller, his only remaining weapon until he knows that he is beaten and without remedy. The ravenous sharks reduce the marlin to a mere skeleton. The old man is very sorry that the fish is not only dead but badly ravished but there is nothing he can do for he acted as an honest fisherman. Santiago steers the skiff towards the harbour where some ignorant tourists mistake the great marlin for a shark. He tells himself that he has gone out too far and hence suffered defeat. Once on the beach, he carries the mast on his shoulders and climbs up the hill wearily to his shack. On his way up he stumbles and falls but rises and plods on. He falls asleep in his shack lying on his face with his arms outstretched and his bruised palms turned up. Manolin comes in the morning and is moved to tears. He nurses Santiago. He says that the old man's luck will turn again and he will then sail with him (Santiago).

As the novel ends, the old man sleeps dreaming of his lions and Manolin sits beside him.

7

Dynamics of Narration

Hemingway's *To Have and Have Not* and *Across the River and into the Trees* are experimental novels. The former leads to the success of *For Whom the Bell Tolls* and the latter to the effective narration of *The Old Man and the Sea.*

To Have and Have Not was not conceived as a novel. The first two parts of the novel had been published as short stories before Hemingway thought of writing a third part and putting the three together to make a novel. In this novel, he experiments with the narrative perspective and interior monologues. Part one, entitled "Spring", is told by Harry Morgan, the protagonist, in the first person. Part two, entitled "Autumn", is told in the third person. Part three, "Winter", opens with Albert's narration in the first person, but Albert dies even before the third part is half way through even as Harry dies before the end of the first part. This does violence to the narrative perspective but the novel serves as a good experiment preparatory to the writing of the next novel, *For Whom the Bell Tolls.*

In the same way, *Across the River and into the Trees* is a good experimental novel leading to the effective narration of the next novel, *The Old Man and the Sea,* which became a run away success and got Hemingway the Pulitzer Prize and the Nobel Prize.

The Gulf Stream, which is the scene of most of the action in *To Have and Have Not,* is the locale of the entire action here, making us hark back to Hemingway's tribute to it in *Green Hills of Africa:*

> ...or when you do something which people do not consider a serious occupation and yet you know, truly, that it is as important and has always been as important as all the things that are in fashion, and when, on the sea, you are alone with it and know that this Gulf Stream you are living with, knowing, learning about, and loving, has moved, as it moves, since before man.... (148-149)

The Old Man and the Sea is a dramatization of this theme. The old man, who lives with, knows, and loves the Gulf Stream, is alone on it struggling with the marlin and the sharks and the stream. All the while, the stream is there, and the old man's struggles on it form a brief episode. The tourists at the Terrace represent the flux of life outside the drama of the old man's heroic struggles on the stream. The contrapuntal theme, which Hemingway has kept in the background so far, finally confronts him and becomes the main subject of a novel. The title of the novel makes this explicit presenting the old man in juxtaposition to the sea—*The Old Man and the Sea*, in which 'and' suggests the juxtaposition.

The narrative situation is reduced to simpler terms than in *Across the River and into the Trees*. In *Across the River and into the Trees*, the narrative focus is on Col. Cantwell from beginning to end even though Renata is also there with him for the major portion. This is an important shift in technique from the preceding work, *For Whom the Bell Tolls*, where it is shifted from Jordan and the bridge to Pilar and her story, Maria and her story, Andres and his adventures, Golz and his predicament, and other situations. This technique of uninterrupted narrative focus on a single character is exploited to the best advantage in Hemingway's next novel, *The Old Man and the Sea*.

The narrative focus in *The Old Man and the Sea* is almost continually on the old man except for one or two minor shifts as in the description of the Mako Shark (89-90). The magnitude of the subject, which involves the "one single, lasting thing—the stream", necessitates the omniscient point of view of narration. The classical unities are observed here, especially the unity of place, which is the Gulf Stream throughout the main action, and that of action, which is continuous and remarkably free from any subordinate plot or action. The unity of time is also there, though in a modified form, limited to three days like in *For Whom the Bell Tolls* and *Across the River and into the Trees*. The undeviating focus on the protagonist and the intensity of action and emotional tension make the division of the novel into chapters not only unnecessary, but virtually impossible, and give it the look of a long short story rather than that of a novel.

This type of undeviating focus on a single character prompts us to hark back to the telephone play of the past and, going back further, to one of the ten varieties of ancient Sanskrit drama called *Bhanam*, in which there is only one character on the stage who acts as if he were speaking to or responding to other characters in the wings.

This intense focus helps in the complete dramatization of the narrative. Hemingway presents the old man, the boy, and the sea in the beginning of the novel and allows the story to unfold itself. As the tempo of the story rises, the omniscient narrator's voice is no longer heard; it becomes the means of showing the action. We become oblivious of the narrator and concentrate on the action. The elimination of the narrator in the interests of dramatization is an important feature of *The Old Man and the Sea*.

Both Cantwell and Santiago are given to dreaming and romanticism. Both dream mostly about places (*Across the River and into the Trees*, p. 123 and *The Old Man and the Sea*, p. 19). But Santiago's dreams form part of the artefact of the novel. His dreams are described in detail in pp. 19-20; in the midst of his struggle with the marlin, he dreams of a vast school of porpoises, of his village, and of the long yellow beach and the pride of lions (72); and the novel concludes with the old man dreaming about the lions. This quality of dreaming and romanticism is linked up with their "informed illusion". Carlos Baker refers to Cantwell's "informed illusion": "Everyday is a new and fine illusion. But you can cut out everything phony about the illusion as though you would cut it out with a straight edge razor" (*The Writer as Artist*, 273). Bickford Sylvestor demonstrates that this "informed illusion" is present in Santiago also by quoting from the first dialogue between the old man and Manolin, and the omniscient narrator's comment that "they went through this fiction everyday" (MFS, 473).

The omniscient narrator tells us during the course of the first dialogue between Santiago and Manolin:

> There was no cast net and the boy remembered when they had sold it. But they went through this fiction everyday. There was no pot of yellow rice and fish and the boy knew this too.... The boy did not know whether yesterday's paper was a fiction too. (11)

A little later, when the boy brings supper, wakes up the old man, and says: "I have not wished to open the container until you were ready", the old man replies that he is ready: "I only needed time to wash" (15). The boy wonders where he washed. The omniscient narrator describes his dreams in vivid detail and comments:

> He no longer dreamed of storms, nor of women, nor of great occurrences, nor of great fish, nor fights, nor contests of strength, nor of his wife. He only dreamed of places now and of the lions on the beach. They played like young cats in the dusk and he loved them as he loved the boy. He never dreamed about the boy. (19-20)

He never dreams about the boy because he does not have to. It is the boy in him that watches the lions on the African beach: "When I was of your age I was before the mast on a square rigged ship that ran to Africa and I have seen lions on the beaches in the evening (17).

This youthful experience is permanently enshrined in his dream-memory. The boy in him thus stays with him and this explains the camaraderie between him and Manolin. Manolin is an outward manifestation of the boy in him, who remains an invisible observer of the beach and the lions and other things in his dreams. During his ordeal, Santiago expresses the wish that he had the boy with him at six different times, and the last time he repeats the wish thrice over with considerable emotion. This happens after the marlin jumps and makes him fall onto the bow with his face in the cut slice of the dolphin. He has been dreaming of the lions on the yellow beach, when the fish jumps and wakes him up rudely. His wish for the boy is associated with the boy in him—a romantic yearning for his youthful strength. Besides, the fact that he is all alone on the limitless expanse of waters also explains his desire to hear human voice, albeit his own, and to have some company on the skiff even if it is a bird. Santiago himself reflects on this matter when he realizes that he is talking aloud (32-33).

Santiago stops wishing for the boy after killing the marlin, which fills him with a sense of guilt, almost fratricidal: "I am a tired old man. But I have killed this fish which is my brother and now I must do the slave work" (84-85). But occasionally he thinks of DiMaggio until the scavenger sharks come and put an end to it. The two images from which he has drawn his supply of inspiration and confidence are no longer available to him. Carlos Baker notes that the boy image, the DiMaggio image and the hand-game-image are used by Santiago to gain confidence, but he returns to the image of the boy most often (*The Writer As Artist*, 305).

The mechanics of narration in this novel consist in giving the reader a clear, objective view of the drama taking place on the sea, while allowing him to involve himself emotionally with what the protagonist thinks and does. As the novel opens, the narrator tells us that Santiago, an old and experienced fisherman, whose hands bear the marks of handling heavy fish, has gone without a fish for eighty-four days, and "every thing about him was old except his eyes", which were sea-blue, cheerful and undefeated (6). This significant exception is related to the existence within Santiago of the boy, who sees the pride of lions on the African beach, and a romanticism which explains his 'informed illusion' and well-understood and innocuous pretension. We learn from Santiago's reflections early in the book that he loves the sea and her denizens, and is gifted with an unusual understanding and compassion. He is sorry for the small birds "that were always flying and looking and almost never finding", wonders why such delicate birds are made when the ocean can be so cruel, and then shows a rare understanding of the cruelty of the ocean also:

> But the old man always thought of her as feminine and as something that gave or withheld great favours, and if she did wild or wicked things, it was because she could not help them. The moon affects her as it does a woman, he thought." (24)

Santiago has overcome the weakness of anger and this is made clear even earlier when we are told by the omniscient narrator that many fishermen in The Terrace "made fun of the old man and he was not angry" (7). Col. Cantwell of *Across the River and into the Trees* is shown in the process of overcoming this weakness and Santiago as completely free from it. Even in his fight with the sharks there is no rancor. He fights like a soldier and admires even the *dentuso* "who is beautiful and noble and knows no fear of anything" (95).

When the old man does not know what he has against him (39), and wonders if it is a marlin or a broadbill or a shark (44), we already have the superior knowledge that it is a marlin one hundred fathoms down in the sea (34). The omniscient narrator gives us a panoramic view of the vast scene as Santiago lies forward "cramping himself against the line with all of his body", and dreams of porpoises and lions: "The moon had been up for a long time but he slept on and the fish pulled on steadily and the boat moved into the tunnel of clouds" (72).

As Santiago looks at the marlin, lashed to the skiff, constantly to make sure that it is all true, and is blissfully ignorant of the approaching Mako shark, we keep track of the movements of the shark as he comes up from deep down in the water, and swims fast and hard on the course of the skiff, sometimes losing the scent and picking it up again (89-90). It is this superior point of view that makes us aware of the tragic irony of Santiago who pities the flying fish and the shark that have little chance. We, with our superior knowledge, know that neither marlin nor dolphin nor shark nor Santiago has any chance against the "one single, lasting thing—the stream".

The emotional tension, which starts rising when the old man feels the pull on the line for the first time, keeps on rising, punctuated by a brief spell of relaxation after each peak, only to be followed by a higher peak of tension. The peaks of tension throughout his struggle with the marlin find their dramatic correlative in the line joining the fisherman and the fish, which becomes so taut that beads of water jump from it and sometimes reaches the very edge of the breaking point and pulls down the old man (44, 48, 73, 74). For some time, Santiago's cramped left hand also serves as a dramatic correlative for the emotional tension in the narrative. When tension reaches its last and highest peak in his struggle with the marlin, Santiago reaches a point when he does not care "who kills who" (82). The brief interlude which follows the kill sees the old man lashing the marlin to the boat, dining on shrimps, and convincing himself that it has all really happened and is not a dream. But the interlude ends when the first shark appears and from this point onwards the emotional tension shows an upward curve. The curve of tension does not decline as it normally does after rising to a peak in accordance with the normal, natural pattern of alternating tension and relaxation; it pauses for a while in its upward journey as the old man waits for more sharks. As the old man shouts "Ay", like one feeling the nail go through his hands, watching the two *Galanos*, the emotional curve resumes its upward journey. It pauses briefly again, without declining, when the two sharks are killed and the old man waits for more to come. In this way, the curve shows only brief pauses in its upward motion until it reaches its climax when Santiago fights the sharks desperately in the dark losing his knife and club and breaking his tiller, his only remaining weapon, and knows that he is beaten finally and without remedy. Carlos Baker thinks that "the basic rhythms of the novel, in its maritime sections, are essentially those of the groundswell of the sea", and a matter of mere "stress-yield, brace-relax alternation" (*The Writer As Artist*, 309). Each stress is followed by a more intense stress unlike the groundswell, which does not have a steadily rising tempo punctuated by brief declensions. The basic rhythm is more like the circles made by the marlin, each circle shorter at a higher level than its predecessor, until, at the end, the marlin rises high out of the water and hangs in the air above the old man before falling dead into the water. The narrative rhythm in *The Old Man and the Sea* is modelled on concentric circles at different rising levels culminating in the tension rising higher and higher, without any declension but only brief pauses, until Santiago's dark, desperate battle with the sharks is over.

Hemingway superimposes a paradox over the obvious ironic pattern of this novel. Santiago catches a giant marlin after eighty-four days of unsuccessful fishing on the high seas only to lose most of it to the sharks. His great triumph is reduced to a miserable failure and what he brings home is only the skeleton of the magnificent fish lashed to his skiff. But this basic irony is transformed into a paradox, when we consider how the old man fights the sharks with an indomitable will and brings home his prize, though in a bad shape, realizes his "hubris", takes the punishment, and achieves true humility, admitting to himself as well as to the boy that he is beaten (107, 112). Material failure is transmuted into moral and spiritual triumph and Santiago suffers a victorious defeat reminding us of Jesus's paradoxes: "Whosoever shall seek to save his life, shall lose it; and whosoever shall lose his life shall preserve it" (St. Luke, 17:33) or "Everyone that exalteth himself shall be abased; and he that humbleth himself shall be exalted" (St. Luke, 18:14).

The prize that he brings home finally is humility. The novel presents the spirit of man struggling not only against the marlin and the sharks, but against pride which is ultimately overcome. The contrapuntal framework of the old man contending against the vast sea and her denizens far out "beyond all people in the world" helps in giving a powerful expression to this thematic paradox. Hemingway makes a skilful use of the techniques of point of view and interior monologue in giving an effective expression to his subject. *The Old Man and the Sea* is an effective expression of Hemingway's basic contrapuntal theme. The story yields to a variety of symbolic interpretations, but these are all new dimensions which the perceptive critic sees. Even if we are prejudiced against symbolic writing and the habit of reading between the lines, we still find that the story, by itself, has an absorbing interest and a powerful appeal. The novel is the best example of Hemingway's unobtrusive art which, without showing itself, does its work on the reader (San O' Faolain, 113). As Robert P. Weeks points out, he confers on a seemingly routine experience affecting ordinary people a cosmic significance (15-16).

8

The Iceberg

In his acceptance message to the Swedish Academy, Hemingway says:

> Things may not be immediately discernible in what a man writes.... And by these, and a degree of alchemy that he possesses, he will endure or be forgotten. (Baker, *The Writer As Artist*, 339)

He believes that if a writer knows what he is writing about and is writing truly enough, he may omit things that he knows and the reader will have a feeling of those things as strongly as though the writer had stated them. He says in *Death in the Afternoon*:

> The dignity of movement of an iceberg is due to only one-eighth of it being above water. (183)

Illustrating this principle to George Plimpton, he explains how he eliminated everything unnecessary to conveying the experience to the reader in *The Old Man and the Sea*, which could have been over a thousand pages long:

> I have seen the marlin mate and know about that. So I leave that out. I have seen a school (or pod) of more than fifty sperm whales in that same stretch of water and once harpooned one nearly sixty feet in length and lost him. So I left that out. All the stories I know from the fishing village I leave out. But the knowledge is what makes the underwater part of the iceberg. (34-35)

The iceberg theory points to the literary technique of suggestion which means implied expression rather than explicit statement, or a subtle hinting at something by creating an impression through suppression. When carried further, it leads to symbolism, a kind of literary expression which is non-transparent and which beckons us beyond the literal meaning to a meaning or meanings lurking elsewhere. Hemingway expresses this in a symbolic way in the following passage:

> ...Nick looked down into the clear, brown water, coloured from the pebbly bottom, and watched the trout keeping themselves steady in the current. As he watched them they changed their positions by quick angles, only to hold steady in the fast water again. Nick watched them a long time.
>
> He watched them holding themselves with their noses into the current, many trout in deep, fast moving water, slightly distorted as he watched far down through the glassy convex surface of the pool, its surface pushing and swelling smooth against the resistance of the log-driven piles of the bridge. At the bottom of the pool were the big trout. Nick did not see them at first. Then he saw them at the bottom of the pool, big trout looking to hold themselves on the gravel bottom in a varying mist of gravel and sand, raised in spurts by the current. ("Big Two-Hearted River: I", *In Our Time*, 178)

Nick Adams, here, is like a student of literature discovering hidden meanings in a work of art. He watches the trout "keeping themselves steady in the current with wavering fins", and then he sees many trout in deep, fast moving water, but does not suspect the presence of the big trout at the bottom. Then they appear to him "in a varying mist of gravel and sand", like symbolic meanings hidden under a lucid style. Nick progresses to this discovery from the easily observable trout in the current, which parallel symbolic referents in literature.

Anything that signifies something else is a symbol, in a broad sense. A concrete thing may connote an abstraction; an event may stand for a complex situation; and a situation may have an anagogic or mystic significance. Symbolistic writing is thought-provoking and makes possible the reader's active participation in the business of literature. Symbolism is like an invisible bridge linking up the seen and the unseen, the known and the unknown. As it functions in this capacity, sometimes, it may have a certain indefiniteness about it, and Edgar Allan Poe has this to say on this subject: "I know that indefiniteness is an element of the true music [of poetry]—I mean of the true musical expression...a suggestive indefiniteness of vague and, therefore, of spiritual effect" (Edmund Wilson, 13). It involves a certain element of introspection, a certain inward searching for truths which seem to be hidden away somewhere in the psyche from our external vision. This is an important strand in the American fictional tradition, the leading lights of which are Hawthorne, Poe, Melville, Mark Twain and James.

Hemingway, the mainstay of whose aesthetics is truthful writing, was taken to be a naturalistic or a realistic writer for a long time. But since Malcolm Cowley placed him on the same shelf with Poe, Hawthorne, and Melville, "the haunted and nocturnal writers, the men who dealt in images that were symbols of an inner world", any number of symbolic meanings have been read into Hemingway's works. It would be a mistake to label Hemingway as a symbolist in the sense Mallarme or Yeats or Kafka is a symbolist. Symbolism is elevated to a cult by Mallarme, one of symbolism's most influential high-priests, and the poets who came under his influence. But when stretched too far, it could cloud the meaning in a work of art and lead to a total mystification of things; or the meaning in the background would overshadow the one in the foreground. Such heavy dependence on symbolistic techniques is ordinarily neither possible nor healthy in fiction, where the narrative in the foreground is of the utmost importance, for, unless it is truthfully and masterfully rendered, the meaning of the writer, which is of primary value, will be lost on the reader.

Hemingway uses symbolistic techniques in a closely controlled way. He scarcely ever loses his control over his writing techniques, just as his protagonists or he himself would handle with the greatest control a gun or a fishing rod or a glass of liquor. But he is quite conscious of the possibility of the symbols carrying more meanings than intended. He is reported to have said:

> No good book has ever been written that has in it symbols arrived at beforehand and stuck in.... That kind of symbol sticks out like raisins in raisin bread.... I tried to make a real old man, a real boy, a real sea and a real fish and real sharks. But if I made them good and true enough they would mean many things. The hardest thing is to make something really true and sometimes truer than true. (*Time*, December 1954, 72)

Hemingway seems to believe that a writer's use of symbolism is always unconscious. He thinks that what a writer makes truthfully may mean many things. A writer may not insert symbols artificially in his work, but, as his conscious mind is occupied with making real things, his unconscious may sort out things in such a way that the things so made have a symbolic or ironic significance and all the writer's intellectual and moral equipment including his training, tradition, and honesty goes into this kind of creation.

It is difficult to agree with Hemingway when he says that in a good book symbols are never arrived at beforehand and stuck in. Hemingway's own practice, at times, does not uphold this view. If he said what he really believed in and practiced, he would not have prefaced "The Snows of Kilimanjaro" with an epigraph containing a reference to the leopard, which has nothing to do with the story, if it is not viewed as a symbol. Hemingway's remarks to interviewers should be taken with a grain of salt, for he never liked to be interviewed and was either impatient or attitudinizing during the interviews. But he is truthful and precise in his writings and his theory of "The Iceberg" throws considerable light on his technique of understatement and symbolism ("The dignity of movement of an iceberg is due to only one-eighth of it being above water").

Symbolism is a kind of understatement. The writer, who consciously uses a symbol, omits certain things and leaves it to the symbol to suggest them. The writer may have a literary allusion in mind, a mythological or religious allusion, or may be very strongly aware of a situation, physical or psychological, but may not say it in so many words and only suggest it by some subtle touch. The allusions in the writer's mind also serve the purpose of lighting up a situation and making the general meaning clear. Symbolism in fiction, like other narrative techniques, should contribute to the general meaning of the story or the novel, and the total functioning of the different narrative devices is of the nature of orchestration, producing the harmony of form in fiction.

The following study of Hemingway's use of symbolism in general and its use in *The Old Man and the Sea* is only a clinical analysis and does not pretend to arrive at any value judgments.

ROMANCE, MYTH AND RITUAL

Gertrude Stein says of Hemingway: "And that is Hemingway, he looks like a modern and he smells of the museums" (216). Stein does not mean this to be a compliment. But this remark illustrates certain aspects of Hemingway's work containing vestiges and echoes of legend, mythology and classical literature.

A course in classical literature in Sylvia Beach's "Shakespeare and Company" formed part of his literary apprenticeship. His close association with writers who were experimenting in new writing techniques including the symbolistic, like Pound, Stein, Joyce, Fitzgerald, and Eliot, two of whom, Joyce and Eliot have made a direct appeal to our sense of myth and romance, might have roused his interest in mythology and legend as potential sources of a kind of allusive writing.

Besides, as heir to the American tradition of Romance and Myth and as one who lived close to the Ojibway Indians in his boyhood, it would be surprising if he remained free from the influence of romance, myth and ritual.

Nick Adams is a direct descendant of Natty Bumppo and Huckleberry Finn. He is less heroic than Natty Bumppo for he does not perform any heroic exploits, and less wild than Huck, who lights out "for the territory ahead" to avoid being civilized. Natty and Huck, though in different ways, resist the lure of civilization and remain frontiersmen. Originally wild, they are initiated into the mysteries of civilization and, in the end, disappear into the wilderness where they belong. But Nick Adams belongs to our world, the civilized world. He goes into the wide world, like a Jason or a Theseus obeying the call of adventure, faces the horrors of pain and death or an ogre of a battler or of a psychic monster like traumatic neurosis or *nada*, and returns. The pattern of his life fits in with that of the mythical hero *mutatis mutandis* in the light of modern conditions:

> A hero ventures forth from the world of common day into a region of supernatural wonder: fabulous forces are there encountered and a decisive victory is won; the hero comes back from this mysterious adventure with the power to bestow boons on his fellow man. (Campbell, 30)

This mythological journey recurs again and again in Hemingway's all novels. But the modern hero's adventure is only with the strange and the fearful; his victory is only survival; and his knowledge is only disillusionment.

A mythical crossing of the waters forms part of the initiation into a new world in "Indian camp". It figures importantly in *A Farewell to Arms, To Have and Have Not, Across the River and into the Trees* and *The Old Man and the Sea*. In *The Sun Also Rises* and *For Whom the Bell Tolls*, it is limited to a symbolic contact with water prior to initiation. It is a kind of baptismal or purificatory rite preparing the hero for the next adventure or marking an important change in his attitude or personality.

The primitive people believed that elaborate ceremonies and rituals helped them in learning to live in harmony with nature. It was a way of acknowledging the supremacy of the abiding earth and living in unison with it. The initiation rites make the whole society visible to itself as an imperishable living unit.

As Joseph Campbell puts it, "Generations of individuals pass, like anonymous cells from a living body; but the sustaining timeless form remains" (383). This is the meaning of the rituals.

As Nick carefully reaches his hand down and takes hold of the hopper by the wings, or as Jake digs for worms on the grassy banks of the stream at Burguete with the goats watching him, or as Frederic Henry reflects on how anger was washed away in the river along with any obligation, or as Robert Jordan holds on to himself very carefully and delicately to keep his hands steady, his heart beating against the pine needles, or as Cantwell shuts the car door carefully and well before his death, or as Santiago keeps his lines straight up and down and at their proper depths, it is of this ritual that we are reminded—the ritual of doing things with a deliberation, imparting an aura of significance to very common actions. Look at Santiago keeping his lines:

> He looked down into the water and watched the lines that went straight down into the dark of the water. He kept them straighter than anyone did, so that at each level in the darkness of the stream there would be a bait waiting exactly where he wished it to be for any fish that swam there. Others let them drift with the current and sometimes they were at sixty fathoms when the fishermen thought they were at a hundred.
>
> But, he thought, I keep them with precision. Only I have no luck any more. But who knows? May be today. Every day is a new day. It is better to be lucky. But I would rather be exact. Then when luck comes you are ready. (26)

This ritualized activity is the formula for the emotion the primitive man felt at the time of the initiation rites and the seasonal rites. It involves an apotheosis of the continual form of the community or the flux of life and of the abiding earth as opposed to the passing generations of individuals. Man who is marked for death from the moment of his birth has to live in harmony with these inevitables of destiny, until he becomes part of the everlasting earth.

Jake of *The Sun Also Rises* is like the Fisher King of the Grail legend, whose wound and impotence symbolize the sterility of a generation. T.S. Eliot uses this motif as well as others in his *The Waste Land*. In this and the primitive ceremonies, as in other references to myth and legend, Hemingway's technique is very close to Eliot's use of the objective correlative for the emotion involved. Only, he seems to be a more rigid symbolist than Eliot, since he not only does not provide the reader with any clue to the meaning but also makes it very difficult for him to detect the symbols, which are generally hidden away under a surface story—truthful depiction of what actually happens and what really produces the surface emotion which is felt. The symbols are there at the bottom like the trout which Nick does not see at first. It takes a discerning reader to discover the symbols hidden under the surface of a deceptively lucid narrative.

Like the Fisher King, whose wound and impotence symbolize the sterility of a generation, Santiago's scarred hands and his going without taking a fish for eighty-four days, reflect a kind of impotence and point to the barrenness of culture and knowledge we find in the tourists towards the end of the novel. Santiago is a Fisher King, for he is a king among fishermen.

The Old Man and the Sea demonstrates a close parallel with the mythical pattern of the hero's separation, initiation and return discussed above. But Santiago is the modern hero of "our times". So, when he returns with his superior knowledge and love after his exciting adventures on the high seas, there are no crowds to welcome him and sing his praises. There is a sad irony in the lot of the modern hero.

RELIGIOUS SYMBOLISM

There is a strong religious streak in Hemingway's fiction even as it is pronounced in Hemingway's life and his intense Catholicism. Hemingway's fiction has a religious theme and he employs symbols including Christological ones.

His fiction up to *For Whom the Bell Tolls* smacks of Old Testament symbolism, myth and ritual having greater importance than in *Across the River and into the Trees* and *The Old Man and the Sea*, which have a predominantly Christian and Christological symbolism. *For Whom the Bell Tolls* acts as a bridge between the first three major novels and the last two novels, published in his lifetime. It is interesting to note that a bridge is the central symbol in *For Whom the Bell Tolls.*

Nicholas Adams is the hero of the group of stories in *In Our Time* and the other Nick stories in *Men without Women* and *Winner Take Nothing.* His surname suggests Adam, an Old Testament name standing for the first man or the generic man. Hemingway's biblical narrative starts with Adam's initiation to a knowledge of birth and death and, later, his fall from the freight train, when he is thrown out by the brakeman. Adam yields place to Jacob in *The Sun Also Rises.* Brett tells him: "You have a hell of a biblical name, Jake." As Jacob wrestled with God until the breaking of the day (Genesis, 32: 24-30), Jake wrestles with his own consciousness. It is difficult to say whether Jake received a blessing in the end like Jacob after his wrestling with God. If a thorough disillusionment is a blessing, Jake receives it at the end in the ironic mode so characteristic of Hemingway. Earl Rovit thinks that the 'blessing' has to do with his powers to endure (149) which find their full flowering in Santiago's character in *The Old Man and the Sea.*

Once the general suggestiveness of Hemingway's titles and proper nouns is accepted, a significant pattern can be traced from Jacob to Santiago or St. James, through Frederic Henry and Robert Jordan. The protagonist's baptism through rain, which is a predominant symbol in *A Farewell to Arms* and which is heightened by his plunge into the Tagliamento and his final walk back in the rain to his hotel, leads us to Jordan. Robert Jordan, whose surname suggests the river that baptized Jesus Christ, stands prominently between Jake and Santiago like the baptizing river which separates Israel (Jacob) and the apostle, St. James.

Jacob of the *Old Testament* proved himself a worthy fighter when he wrestled with God till the breaking of the day:

"And he said, Thy name shall be called no more Jacob, but Israel: for as a prince hast thou power with God and with men, and hast prevailed" (Genesis, 32: 28). The kind of love expounded by the priest in *A Farewell to Arms* ("when you love, you wish to do things for. You wish to sacrifice for. You wish to serve" [75]) begins to bloom in *For Whom the Bell Tolls*. Mythological symbols yield place to religious and Christological symbols. The rain in *A Farewell to Arms*, which is generally interpreted as a symbol of disaster and death, is a symbol of baptism also. Suffering is the best kind of baptism, and rain, which is associated with suffering and tragedy, dominates the novel. This novel-length baptism finds a personification in Robert Jordan, who represents its flowering by his sense of love, which rises above lust and passion, and by his martyrdom. It is significant that rain does not figure in the last three novels published during Hemingway's lifetime. Its purpose served as an instrument of baptism, rain is no longer needed, and the Christological figure peeps out occasionally through Cantwell and frequently through Santiago, who, at the end, becomes identified with it.

Mary is a recurring religious symbol in *For Whom the Bell Tolls*. This emphasizes the religious symbolism in the novel. The heroine's name, Maria, suggests the Virgin. Her violation is a sacrilege and it symbolizes the curse on Spain. The Fascists' christening of her, in mockery, as the "Bride of the Red Christ", and the cruelties and humiliations heaped upon her prior to the outrage remind us of the ill-treatment meted out to Jesus before the crucifixion. Her recuperation in three days with the aid of the Christian virtue of love is a parallel to the resurrection. It is to Virgin Mary that the appeal is made each time. Joaquin switches over to "Hail Mary" from Passionaria's motto before his death; Lt. Berrendo prays to the Virgin for his dead friend; Anselmo prays to her on seeing the enemy column returning with the severed heads of El Sordo and his men; the letter in the pocket of the Fascist cavalry man killed by Robert Jordan contains a reference to the Blessed Virgin of Pilar.

Apart from its Dantesque metaphor which has a religious tinge of its own, *Across the River and into the Trees* has a biblical hue too. Colonel Cantwell, the protagonist, spends the last three days of his life in Venice, charging them with love and forgiveness, the two great Christian virtues—love for Venice, for Renata, for Gran Maestro, and for everybody he meets and everything he touches, and forgiveness of the boatman who offends him. He is self-critical when he has spoken badly about others and makes a conscious effort, though he knows how hard it is, not to be bitter about things. His one bad hand, which Renata loves much, is like the nailed hand of Jesus.

The Old Man and the Sea has more biblical flavour than any other work by Hemingway. Santiago is the Spanish name of St. James. He is called 'the best fisherman' by Manolin, the boy who admires the old man and loves him. Jesus taught Peter, Andrew, John and James how to 'catch men' instead of catching fishes. He gave them a new life and made saints out of ordinary fishermen. The same kind of conversion comes to Santiago, who is like any other fisherman in the beginning.

The Christological element can be seen not only in Santiago but also in the marlin. Bickford Sylvester points out the parallel between the marlin's death and the crucifixion. The marlin's strange death occurs at noon and Santiago had an unforgettable vision of it. Sylvester says: "It is, perhaps, worth remembering also that while Christ did not die at noon, His ordeal began then, as does the marlin's and that the observers of his death also had a strange vision (PMLA, 135). Let us compare these passages: The old man drove his harpoon 'into the fish's side'.

> Then the fish came alive with his death in him, and rose high out of the water showing all his great length and width and all his power and his beauty. He seemed to hang in the air above the old man in the skiff. Then he fell into the water with a crash that sent spray over the old man and over all of the skiff. (84-85)

This calls up the vision of Jesus on the cross high up in the air with a spear piercing his side (St. John, 19 : 34).

The Christological symbolism moves back and forth between the marlin and Santiago. The marlin is nailed (harpooned) first and lashed to the wood of the boat. As for Santiago, there is a vivid image of the old man as he settled against the wood of the bow, and took his suffering as it came, telling himself 'Rest gently now against the wood and think of nothing' (58). Carlos Baker, Melvin Backman and several other Hemingway critics have written about the crucifixion imagery in the novel in detail.

Santiago's wounded hands, the dried blood on his face, his climbing up the road with the mast on his shoulder, his falling under its weight and the way he lies in his shack "with his arms out straight and the palms of his hands up"—all remind us vividly of the crucifixion episode. Joseph Waldmeir calls our attention to the biblical numerology in the novel—the old man fishing with the boy for *forty* days and then fishing alone for *forty-four* days, struggling with the marlin for *three* days, and landing him on the *seventh* attempt, killing sharks and resting *seven* times. Santiago's return in three days from the death-like sea parallels resurrection. The three-day span in each of the last three novels, published during his life-time, looks like the Christological entombment symbol.

The religious symbols employed by Hemingway are biblical echoes voicing the author's faith and acting as symbolistic devices. They can be seen from his first important work, *In Our Time*, which shows the influence of the prayer, "Give peace in our time, O Lord" of the book of common prayer, through some of his subsequent works like *The Sun Also Rises*, which carries a quotation from *The Ecclesiastes* as one of its epigraphs, and *A Farewell to Arms*, which centres round the gospel of love taught by the preacher, and *For Whom the Bell Tolls*, the title of which is taken from John Donne's devotion, "No man is an island etc., to *The Old Man and the Sea*, in which there is a preponderance of the Christological elements like love, forgiveness, and compassion, apart from explicit biblical imagery as we have just seen in the marlin and Santiago locked in a mortal combat. The religious streak in

Hemingway has consistently made itself manifest in his writings in the form of religious symbolism.

Sylvia Beach says that she has always felt that Hemingway was a deeply religious man (87). He was a devout catholic. He went to churches and prayed. He read *The Old Testament Narratives*, when a school boy, as part of his study course. The Bible was a powerful influence on his thinking and writing. He went to the extent of presenting his Nobel Prize Medal to the shrine of 'Neustra de la Caridad del Cobre' or 'Virgin del Cobre' near Santiago in Cuba in 1956 two years after receiving it. There is a reference to this Church in *The Old Man and the Sea*, during Santiago's epic battle with the giant marlin, when he makes a vow to the Virgin in addition to his prayers:

> 'I am not religious,' he said. 'But I will say ten our Fathers and ten Hail Marys that I should catch this fish, and I promise to make a pilgrimage to the Virgin de Cobre if I catch him. That is a promise.'
>
> He commenced to say his prayers mechanically. Sometimes he would be so tired that he could not remember the prayer and then he would say them fast so that they would come automatically. Hail Marys are easier to say than Our Fathers, he thought.
>
> 'Hail Mary full of Grace the Lord is with thee. Blessed art thou among women and blessed is the fruit of thy womb, Jesus. Holy Mary, Mother of God, pray for us sinners now and at the hour of our death. Amen.' Then he added, 'Blessed Virgin, pray for the death of this fish. Wonderful though he is.' (56-57)

Santiago says, "I am not religious" but says his prayers and vows to make a pilgrimage to the Virgin's Shrine.

In his shack, he has a picture in colour of the Sacred Heart of Jesus and another of the Virgin of Cobre. These were relics of his wife. Once there had been a tinted photograph of his wife on the wall but he had taken it down because it made him too lonely to see it and it was on the shelf in the corner under his clean shirt. (11)

The only female character in *The Old Man and the Sea* is Santiago's wife, who appears as an old tinted photograph hidden away in a corner of the room. She is the repository of his religion and she now exists only as an old photograph but the two relics, the pictures of the Sacred Heart of Jesus and the Virgin de Cobre, symbolize the good woman and her values and faith. While the picture of his wife gives him a sense of bereavement and makes him feel lonely, the pictures of Virgin Mary and the Sacred Heart of Jesus comfort him and strengthen his heart and hence his prayers to them during his struggle with the great marlin.

Thus *The Old Man and the Sea* marks the maturity of Hemingway's religious symbolism.

PSYCHOLOGICAL SYMBOLISM

There have been many attempts to read Freudian and Jungian meanings into Hemingway's fiction. The psychoanalytical method throws new light on certain situations and reveals certain meanings, though it could be, sometimes, stretched too far. Psychological symbolism, in a work of art, is the critic's concern rather than the writer's, for it involves the writer's unconscious as well as the characters, and the writer is generally not conscious of it when he uses it, and, conscious or unconscious, he is, sometimes, caught in his own trap, for the critic may probe the writer's unconscious as well.

Jake of *The Sun Also Rises*, who is rendered impotent by a war wound, thinks of Brett and cries in his bed at night. Brett is a nymphomaniac, and finds comfort in other men's arms while remaining hopelessly and helplessly in love with Jake. Jake suffers all this sorrow and humiliation like T.S. Eliot's Tiresias.

The predicament of Jake and Brett, which is central to *The Sun Also Rises*, finds a striking parallel in the *Corrida de Toros*. Brett is the 'Vaquilla' or the female of the fighting bull and Jake the 'Cabestro' or the trained steer. The three bulls in the ring, Mike, Cohn and Romero make fools of themselves over the Vaquilla, and it is given to Jake, the 'Cabestro' to quiet them and maintain a liaison between one bull and another, and between them and the outside world. Robert W. Lewis, Jr. (32-33) and Dewey Ganzel (26—48) discuss this in great detail. The phallic symbol in the sword of the statue of Marshal Ney and the raised baton of the mounted policeman at the end of the novel has attracted wide critical attention.

The episode of the purchase of the pistol and cartridges in *A Farewell to Arms* (154-155), makes us hark back to the opening chapter in which the marching troops, with cartridge boxes bulging under their capes, looking like pregnant ladies, serve as a dramatic correlative for the story of Frederick and Catherine, who carries in her womb the cartridge that will eventually kill her.

In *The Old Man and the Sea*, when Santiago's phallic harpoon penetrates the marlin so deep that he feels the marlin's heart, he does not merely kill, but achieves a union beyond sex and identifies himself with the fish.

The sleeping bag in *For Whom the Bell Tolls*, the blanket in the gondola in *Across the River and into the Trees*, and the sea in *The Old Man and the Sea* are interpreted as womb symbols indicating a desire for regression into the womb with the sea being referred to as *la mar* or the eternal feminine sea. Earl Rovit advances this interpretation (66). After this kind of interpretation, it is difficult to understand what cannot be considered a womb symbol. John Killinger calls the sea "a primordial womb symbol" (66). To make the vast limitless ocean a womb symbol is to stretch psycho-analysis too far.

Psycho-analytical criticism is a slippery playground, and though the kind of interpretation is quite possible and could be reasonable to some extent, the symbols attributed to the writer may be outside the pale of his conscious technique. The critics, however, can throw light on the writers' unconscious, and by discerning new meanings, can enjoy themselves and enlighten others, for theirs is a job of reconstructing the writer's vision, and they may sometimes see more than the creative writer.

OTHER FORMS OF SYMBOLISM: OBJECTIVE AND DRAMATIC CORRELATIVES

Some names and titles in Hemingway's fiction have a symbolic or ironic significance. The conscious craftsman that he was, he gave meaningful names to some of his characters with a special intent.

Thus, Jake Barnes is a barren Jacob representing the wasteland of a past generation; Pilar is the Blessed Virgin of Pilar, the Mother Figure for the Christ-Surrogates, Maria and Jordan, and the guerillas. Jordan is the river that baptized Jesus and links the Jews and the Muslims, and Robert Jordan is the link between the guerillas and the outside world, and also between Jacob and Santiago; Richard Cantwell, once referred to as Richard, the Lion-Hearted, suffers from a bad heart and cannot get well; Renata or "the reborn", a sort of presiding genius of Venice, is Venus reborn, as her portrait suggests, and also Cantwell's youth reborn; Jackson by nominal association with Stonewall Jackson suggests the death of a perfect soldier, i.e., Col. Cantwell; Manolin, the alter ego of Santiago, is Manolo or Manuel Garcia, the undefeated bullfighter in the story "Undefeated", who is incarnated as Santiago, the undefeated fisherman—a lesser Saint James.

A T.S. Eliot type of allusiveness, achieved through playing with quotations can be seen in some of Hemingway's titles like *In Our Time* from *The Book of Common Prayer, The Sun Also Rises* from *Ecclesiastes, For Whom the Bell Tolls* from one of John Donne's Devotions, and several of his short stories like "The Light of the World" from "St. John" in *The New Testament* or "In Another Country" from Marlowe's *The Jew of Malta* or "Now I Lay Me" from the well-known prayer originally printed in *The New England Primer* (1781).

Rain is an important symbol for suffering and sorrow in *A Farewell to Arms* and in the short story, "Cat in the Rain", which puts us in mind of "Catherine in the rain".

Carlos Baker draws our attention to the "Mountain vs Plain" symbol in *A Farewell to Arms.* He relates these two images to the opposed concepts of Home and Not-Home. The

Home concept is associated with the mountains, with dry, cold weather, with peace, love, dignity, health, happiness and the good life, and with the consciousness of God. The Not-Home concept is associated with low-lying plains, with rain and fog, with obscenity, indignity, disease, war and death, and with irreligion (*The Writer As Artist*, 102).

The "Mountain vs Plain" symbol is an integral symbol which has an important bearing on the meanings of not only *A Farewell to Arms* but also *The Sun Also Rises, For Whom the Bell Tolls,* and "The Snows of Kilimanjaro". In *The Old Man and the Sea* also, there is a significant ascent made by Santiago to his shack. The mountain by its very elevation symbolizes the apotheosis of the abiding earth which serves as a backdrop, like the Gulf Stream, for the human drama presented by Hemingway in novel after novel.

The symbolism of no other fictional work in modern times is, perhaps, more widely interpreted than that of *The Old Man and the Sea.* Stewart Sanderson calls the novel "a sustained and continuous performance in the realm of symbolism", and interprets it as an allegory of the artist's struggle with his art as well as of man's struggle with life: "It is possible to see Hemingway himself with his lines set accurately at various depths, sailing out into the Gulf Stream to land his biggest fish after the technical failures of *Across the River and into the Trees*" (114, 117). Andre Maurois (48) and Philip Young (275) see in the novel a personal allegory in which the marlin stands for *Across the River and into the Trees* and the sharks for the critics who attacked it.

Carlos Baker sees in it a philosophical symbolism, with the Spanish main symbolizing "that more extensive main, or main stream, where we all drift or sail, with or against the wind, in fair weather or foul, with our prize catches and our predatory sharks, and each of us, perhaps, like the ancient mariner of Coleridge, with some kind of albatross round his neck" (*The Writer As Artist*, 311).

Clinton S. Burhans sees a message in favour of team spirit, solidarity and love, as opposed to isolated individualism, in the symbols of DiMaggio, the pride of lions, and the Christological parallel (264).

For Keiichi Harada, Santiago's act represents "*hubris*" rather than sin and the sharks stand for 'Devouring Time' (275-276).

The damaged condition of the marlin, when it is brought ashore, is a mark of the struggle endured by the artist in the process. Mark Schorer explains this symbolism thus:

> It is an old man catching a fish, yes; but it is also a great artist writing about the struggle. Nothing is more important than his craft, and it is beloved; but because it must be struggled with and mastered, it is also a foe, enemy to all self-indulgence, to all looseness of feeling, all laxness of style, all soft pomposities. (134)

The symbolism of the novel can also be explained meaningfully in terms of Shelley's 'fading coal' theory of creative imagination and composition. *The Old Man and the Sea* may be interpreted as a novel-length illustration of Shelley's interesting and highly romantic theory of poetic composition. The great marlin Santiago catches and lashes to his skiff is like the original inspiration while the poor skeleton of it, after the sharks attack it, is like the actual poetic composition, which is a poor feeble shadow of the original vision or inspiration, which fired the poet's imagination originally.

Shelley says:

> A man cannot say 'I will compose poetry'. The greatest poet even cannot say it; for the mind in creation is as a fading coal, which some invisible influence like an inconstant wind, awakens to transitory brightness.... When composition begins, inspiration is already on the decline, and the most glorious poetry that has ever been communicated to the world is probably a feeble shadow of the original conceptions of the poet. (53-54)

Here is the evidence of a poet on how a poem is composed. According to Shelley, the poet's inspiration fades away gradually as he composes. There is an element of sadness of rendering the poetic vision or inspiration, which causes an ecstasy, into a linguistic artefact. Shelley says in his *Ode to the Skylark*:

> Our sweetest songs are those
> That tell of the saddest thought.

This sadness may have something to do with the fact that the poem is 'but a feeble shadow of the original conception of the poet', which is the result of a divine inspiration or *Rasa*, which, according to the *Vedas*, is the same as the Supreme Being (*Raso Vy Saha);* hence the sadness which follows the vanished vision—spiritual enlightenment comes in a flash like a flash of lightning (*Tatidiva bodhodayati*). So does a mystic or poetic vision or inspiration of a high order and, in the process of giving it a linguistic shape, the original inspiration fades away in a large measure like a beautiful dream or a poetic or prose composition conceived in our minds before falling asleep, fading away when we sit down to write on waking up like Santiago's great marlin, eaten away by the sharks of time, or the wonderful dreams of our early life reduced to feeble shadows or skeletons in later life.

Thus *The Old Man and the Sea* means many things to many people. Hemingway seems to have the last word on the subject: "I suppose there are symbols since critics keep finding them.... Read anything I write for the pleasure of reading it. Whatever else you find will be the measure of what you brought to the reading" (Plimpton, 29).

9

A Prose That Has Never Been Written

Hemingway sets forth his ambition to achieve a style in his talk with Kandisky in *Green Hills of Africa:*

> The kind of writing that can be done. How far prose can be carried, if one is serious enough and has luck. There is a fourth and fifth dimension that can be gotten.... It is much more difficult than poetry. It is a prose that has never been written. But it can be written without tricks and without cheating. With nothing that will go bad afterwards. (26-27)

Hemingway had already been famous for his style when he made the above observations. It is important to notice his statement that such a prose had never been written. Obviously, he thought that there were certain dimensions yet to be achieved in his prose. He does not make any claim for himself in this passage, but only points to the possibility of achieving those extra dimensions in writing. That he was trying to achieve something new is clear from the difference in style between his novels written before and after *Green Hills of Africa.*

It shall be my endeavour to examine his style in the light of his ambition to write a prose with new dimensions and his aesthetics of truthful depiction. The latter comes very close to Joseph Conrad's method of putting down what he saw and never what his intellect inferred. Conrad and Hemingway share their attitude to style also to words which have been carelessly and loosely used for generations and to the magic of suggestiveness. Thus Conrad says in his preface to *The Nigger of the 'Narcissus' and Other Tales*:

> ... It is only through an unremitting never-discouraged care for the shape and ring of sentences that an approach can be made to plasticity, to colour, and that the light of magic suggestiveness may be brought to play for an evanescent instant over the common place surface of words: of the old, old words, worn thin, defaced by ages of careless usage. (5)

These ideas find an echo in Hemingway's *Death in the Afternoon*, in which the writer tells the old lady: "Madam, all our words from loose using have lost their edge, but your inherent concepts are most sound" (72).

'Style' for Hemingway always meant the right way to do things as in killing a bull or tracking a wild beast or catching a marlin or taking pain or death. He is reported by *Time* thus:

> The right way to do it—style—is not just an idle concept ... it is simply the way to get done what is supposed to be done. The fact that the right way also looks beautiful when it's done is just incidental. (72)

His interest in creating a style for himself showed itself even during his early school days at Oak Park and his early apprentice years on the staff of the *Kansas City Star*. Therefore, it is not right to say, as Philip Young does, that his style was developed and perfected in the same period when the author was reorganizing his personality after his traumatic experience in Italy. Look at the use of the declarative simple sentence and the technique of repetition, both of which became a hallmark of the famous Hemingway style, in the following passage from "Sepi Jingan" published in the November 1916 issue of the *Tabula*:

> Yes. He was a bad Indian. Up on the upper peninsula, he couldn't get drunk. He used to drink all day—everything. But he couldn't get drunk. Then he would go crazy; but he wasn't drunk. He was crazy because he couldn't get drunk.

Hemingway's trauma of 1918 certainly played an important part in his apprenticeship, as did a number of other factors, but its importance should not be exaggerated. He thought deeply about the problem of depiction and made sincere efforts to cut out the unnecessary details and sentiments clouding the essentials that made the emotion. It was a drive towards masculinity and simplicity unknown to literary writing, and has sharply divided the contemporary critical world into admirers and detractors. Max Eastman ridiculed it as a literary style of wearing false hair on the chest (71). Edwin Berry Burgum called it a stylization of the proletarian speech (314), and Leon Edel described it as "an artifice, a series of charming tricks, a group of cleverness [sic]—only an effect of style by a process of evasion (170).

In contrast, glowing tributes are paid by admirers. H.E. Bates says that Hemingway sheared away the literary woolliness of English as no one had ever done before (72). Philip Young regards him as the greatest prose stylist next to Thoreau in American literature, at the most, and, at the very least, the writer of some of the cleanest, freshest, subtlest, most brilliant and most moving prose of our time" (173). Wright Morris sees Hemingway's style as an expression of the age itself, hears the far sound of running water and feels a pine-scented breeze blowing from a cleaner and finer world (135-136). Archibald Macleish sings in *Time*:

> Veteran out of the wars before he was twenty:
> Famous at twenty-five; thirty a master—
> Whittled a style for his time from a walnut stick
> In a carpenter's loft in a street of the April City. (70)

A deep investigation of Hemingway's style reveals two styles—one evocative, lyrical, and tender, and the other depictive, hard-boiled, and masculine, as pointed out and discussed in detail by Charles R. Anderson (41-46). This dichotomy corresponds to the contrapuntal theme, which is central to Hemingway's narrative work—the human drama versus the everlasting earth, horological time counterpointed by geological time. The abiding earth or the great Gulf Stream, against the background of which all human effort is ineffectual, demands a tight-lipped, well-honed, masculine prose, while the human drama requires an evocative, romantic, tender prose to express its poignancy. The style is best suited to Hemingway's theme of Aphrodite locked inescapably in the arms of Ares—the tender, evocative, poetic style wrapped in the embrace of the rugged simplicity of the staccato sentences. At the back of this dualistic style is the incongruous personality of Hemingway himself, beautifully captured by *The New Yorker* cartoon which shows a brawny, muscle-knotted forearm and a hairy hand clutching a rose, entitled "The Soul of Ernest Hemingway", referred to by Robert Penn Warren in his introduction to *A Farewell to Arms* (xxi).

THE CULT OF SIMPLICITY

The cult of simplicity is not a novelty in English Prose. The authorized version of the Bible has set the pace for it. Hemingway belongs to this stylistic tradition of simplicity. His preference for concrete words, unencumbered by merely decorative qualifiers, intensifiers, and figures of speech, can be seen in the following passage from *The Old Man and the Sea:*

> He started to climb again and at the top he fell and lay for sometime with the mast across his shoulder. He tried to get up. But it was too difficult and he sat there with the mast on his shoulder and looked at the road. (109)

Here is no effort to introduce emotion, but only a bare action-picture of what happened—the picture which is the formula of the emotion one feels. The simplest possible words are used and the active verb is the simple past—'started', 'fell', 'lay', 'tried', 'sat', and 'looked'. The passage being an action-picture, the verb is the important word. There is one simple sentence and two compound sentences made up of three simple sentences in each case and joined by 'and'. The technique of 'polysyndeton' with 'and' as the most frequently used conjunction is a favourite technique with Hemingway and survives some of his stylistic changes into *The Old Man and the Sea.* It makes the verbal action-picture more fast, simple sentence after simple sentence running in quick succession, the copula, 'and', audibly as well as visibly holding the different units of the picture together. Look at another passage from *The Old Man and the Sea:*

> Blood came out from under the finger-nails of both his and the negro's hands and they looked each other in the eye and at their hands and forearms and the bettors went in and out of the room and sat on high chairs against the wall and watched. (60-61)

The absence of punctuation and the coordinate 'and' help in leading the reader from one picture to another without any pause until the whole picture hangs as one unit before his eyes. The copula is the non-interfering commentator's voice, now reduced to the minimum. The pictures are simply presented one by one without any commentary on their relative importance and without subordinating one image to another. 'And' helps in this kind of presentation which frequently is of the nature of cinematography. Joseph Warren Beach terms this "the great leveling democracy of the 'and'" (101).

THE TECHNIQUE OF REPETITION

Repetition as a stylistic device is used to the maximum advantage by Hemingway. This technique could be traced back to his freshman text of *Old Testament Narratives*. Hemingway captures the incantatory effect of the repetition of 'and' so profusely used in the Bible, especially in *The Old Testament.* It transforms language into a kind of verbal ritual, completely in keeping with the ritualistic action with its emphasis on the form—doing things carefully, correctly, as if the form were everything. Ritual is formal homage or worship or glorification. The everlasting earth and the great Gulf Stream representing nature and the flux of life, against which man cannot prevail, draw homage from Hemingway, and the ritualistic style is the form this homage seems to take:

> He looked down into the water and watched the lines that went straight down into the dark of the waters. He kept them straighter than anyone did, so that at each level in the darkness of the stream there would be a bait

> waiting exactly where he wished it to be for any fish that swam there. Others let them drift with the current and sometimes they were at sixty fathoms when the fishermen thought they were at a hundred. (26)

Santiago's carefulness, precision and his correct way of doing things can be seen in the above passage.

The old man says ten 'Our Fathers' and ten 'Hail Marys' in a mechanical manner. Prayers are repetitive and repetition lends strength to the prayer or the thought as is the case in hypnotism.

A tired and beaten Santiago thinks of rest and the word 'bed' is repeated four times:

> The wind is our friend, any way, he thought. Then he added, sometimes. And the great sea with our friends and our enemies. And bed, he thought. Bed is my friend. Just bed, he thought. Bed will be a great thing. It is easy when you are beaten, he thought. (108)

His dreams of the lions on the beach are also repeated and when the novel closes, he is dreaming about them.

A tired and sleepless Santiago, fearing he might become unclear in the head if he does not sleep says:

> I'm clear enough in the head, he thought. Too clear. I am as clear as the stars that are my brothers. Still I must sleep. They sleep and the moon and the sun sleep and even the ocean sleeps sometimes on certain days when there is no current and a flat calm.
>
> But remember to sleep, he thought. Make yourself do it and devise some simple and sure way about the lines. (68)

The words 'clear' and 'sleep' are repeated again and again as Santiago makes an auto-suggestion to his mind giving commands to keep clear and alert and still try to get a little sleep.

Thus repetition and the repeated use of 'and' lend an incantatory effect to the style. They cast a spell on the reader even as they throw light on the situation. They also help in depicting sensations effectively.

THE TWO STYLES

Hemingway's style is generally a highly controlled style unaffected by its duality which is subject to the general discipline of the style. One strand of his dual style rests mainly on literary allusions harking back nostalgically to the Elizabethans, for the most part, and the method is Eliotean, evoking the mood or the emotion associated with the quotation or the allusion employed.

The best example for the poetic strand in Hemingway's dualistic style is the one from *A Farewell to Arms* cited and analysed by Charles R. Anderson (204-205).

The usual hard-boiled staccato style and the clipped dialogue operate check by jowl with the romantic, lyrical style in Hemingway's later novels. In the short stories and early novels, the hard-boiled, realistic style with its staccato sentences dominates, while in the later novels, *The Old Man and the Sea* in particular, there is a harmonious union between the two styles. This can be seen when we take a close look at the opening paragraphs of *The Old Man and the Sea*:

> He was an old man who fished alone in a skiff in the Gulf Stream and he had gone eighty-four days now without taking a fish. In the first forty days a boy had been with him. But after forty days without a fish the boy's parents had told him that the old man was now definitely and finally *salao*, which is the worst form of unlucky, and the boy had gone at their orders in another boat which caught three good fish the first week. It made the boy sad to see the old man come in each day with his skiff empty and he always went down to help him carry either the coiled lines or the gaff and harpoon and the sail that was furled around the mast. The sail was patched with flour sacks and, furled, it looked like the flag of permanent defeat.
>
> The old man was thin and gaunt with deep wrinkles in the back of his neck. The brown blotches of the

> benevolent skin cancer the sun brings from its reflection on the tropic sea were on his cheeks. The blotches ran well down the sides of his face and his hands had the deep-creased scars from handling heavy fish on the cords. But none of these scars were fresh. They were as old as erosions in a fishless desert.
>
> Everything about him was old except his eyes and they were the same colour as the sea and were cheerful and undefeated. (5-6)

The opening chapters of Hemingway's first two novels are characterized by irony and humour. But here there is neither irony nor humour, but only pathos and poetry. The prose is not completely conventional and is characteristic of the later Hemingway. The foreign word, *salao*, testifies to this. The vocabulary of discrimination, a very useful phrase used by David Lodge (99), is more subtly employed here to evoke a mood of pathos: old man, alone, *salao*, sad, empty, permanent defeat, wrinkles, blotches, scars, and fishless. The language is deliberately suggestive with 'forty' repeated twice, reminding us of the forty days Jesus spends in the wilderness after his baptism. Forty could also be an allusion to the wanderings of the Israelites for forty years before reaching the promised land. The presence of poetic images like "the flag of permanent defeat" and "erosions in a fishless desert" is uncharacteristic of the early Hemingway, but for exceptional cases. So is the alliteration in "brown blotches of the benevolent skin cancer the sun brings from its reflection on the tropic sea". The close repetition of 'b' in the first part of the sentence and the spaced repetition of 's' in the second part shows that greater attention is paid to the ear and the melody of the sentence than before, and this is done without any injury to the rhythm of the sentence by a careful spacing of the alliterative sounds—the third 'b' separated from the second by two syllables, the second 's' from the first 's' by three syllables, and the third 's' from the second 's' by ten syllables, thereby avoiding monotony.

The description of the features of the old man is significant. Though it is not detailed and vivid, it is imagistic and poetic. 'Gaunt', 'thin', 'brown blotches', how they run down the sides of his face, and the scars on his hands are part of an impressionistic picture which is completed by a description of his eyes, which were the same colour as the sea and cheerful and undefeated.

The passage sets the pace in language to the rest of the novel, the main emotions of which are pathos and compassion. It shows how the clean bare understatement of the early works is slightly toned up so as to include a little poetic feeling, and the lyricism considerably toned down so as to merge into the general rhythm of the new style. The allusions to mythology and classical literature, which are part of the style in the early novels and which become banal and wearisome in *Across the River and into the Trees,* are conspicuously absent in *The Old Man and the Sea.* The two styles meet and merge in the novel. This is made possible by narrowing down the range further than in *Across the River and into the Trees*, and working more skilfully in depth.

The two styles keep apart, at different levels, in the first two novels in which the contrapuntal theme is most pronounced, and the protagonist is baffled and helpless. Irony is the main tone of these two novels indicating the gap or the strange relationship between incongruities. But the style undergoes a change after *Green Hills of Africa*: and the protagonist becomes less and less baffled until he grows into the wise old Santiago; irony withers away yielding place to paradox; and the prose aspires to the condition of poetry as the protagonist progresses from sex and violence to love and compassion.

As Harry Levin observes, "The paradox of toughness and sensitivity is resolved, and the qualities and defects of his writing are reconciled, if we merely remember that he was—and still is—a poet" (608). The process of reconciliation starts with *For Whom the Bell Tolls,* suffers a setback in *Across the River and into the Trees*, and is completed in *The Old Man and the Sea.*

THE EXTRA DIMENSIONS

Hemingway says, in his conversation with Kandisky in *Green Hills of Africa* that there is a fourth and fifth dimension that can be gotten (26-27). The fourth dimension, in general, is said to be 'time', and if at all Hemingway meant the fourth dimension seriously, it could be his manipulation of the time-element in fiction in novel ways. But it is more probable that Hemingway referred to the fourth and fifth dimensions as new dimensions which it is possible to achieve in prose, and not to any two definite dimensions he had in mind. He himself consciously experimented with prose patterns and might have felt that it was possible to discover new dimensions.

Hemingway's handling of the time-element could be one of them; his evocation of metaphor without making any suggestion whatsoever, but only by bare factual depiction of events may be another; his usage of repetition to evoke an emotion or atmosphere may be yet another; his achievement of a kind of poetic writing without recourse to any poetic device as in *The Old Man and the Sea* may also be a new dimension. His heavy dependence on the interior monologue in his post-*Green Hills of Africa* novels as also his frequent shifting of the narrative point of view in *For Whom the Bell Tolls* to telescope past action (Pilar and Maria's accounts) and parallel action (Andre's journey to Golz's headquarters) may also be interpreted as new dimensions.

Hemingway's reference to the fourth and fifth dimensions raised a lot of controversy. The dust has not yet settled. Some critics have claimed that Hemingway has achieved the fourth and fifth dimensions while others have ridiculed the claim and debunked Hemingway. F.I. Carpenter believes that Hemingway has achieved not only the fourth but the fifth dimension as well. He points out that Hemingway often discussed his art with his mentor, Gertrude Stein, a trained philosopher and a former pupil of William James, whose philosophy of 'radical empiricism' ('immediate' or 'pure' experience) influenced Bergson, who emphasized the difference between psychological time and physical time, and P.D. Ouspensky, who used the expression, 'fifth dimension' and defined it as a 'Line of perpetual now' in 'A New Model of the Universe' in 1931. Carpenter concludes that Hemingway's fifth dimensional prose has attempted to communicate the immediate experience of 'the perpetual now' (193). Michael F. Meloney contends that Hemingway's prose not only lacks a fourth and fifth dimension but, for the most part, a third also, and finds fault with his failure to make his naturalism link up with the world of spirit giving evidence to that potential in man which either raises him above or sinks him below the rest of the animal world (191). Malcolm Cowley, a great friend and admirer of Hemingway says that any good prose has four dimensions, in the sense of being a solid object that moves through time, "whereas the fifth dimension is here a mystical or meaningless figure of speech" (47).

Thus critics, through their manipulation of language, can interpret, justify, negate or dismiss literary concepts and claims.

10

Characterization

SANTIAGO

When the narrative focus is intensely turned on a character, as in the case of Santiago, we tend to lose sight of some aspects of his character. In *The Old Man and the Sea*, the focus is almost continuously on Santiago with the result that our judgment is clouded in some measure. But when we manage to overcome this problem and gain a clear vision and look at the character unblinkingly and open-mindedly, we discover that he has some strong prejudices and if we contemplate these prejudices attentively, we come to the conclusion that they boil down to a single prejudice—gender prejudice.

The first instance in this regard is his attitude to his wife who is no more. He has taken down her old photograph from a wall and put it away on the shelf "in the corner under his clean shirt" (11). He does not think even once of his wife during his struggle against the marlin and sharks. His relegation of her photo to an obscure corner suggests an attempt to erase her memory. This may be interpreted as a dislike of some aspects of his marital life which might have held unpleasant memories for him, and not a general gender prejudice. But his vilification of a jellyfish, the Portuguese man-of-war, shows his prejudice against women in general. As a man-of-war bird circles above dolphins and flying fish trying to hunt the flying fish, Santiago commends "his" efforts and regards "him" a great help, for "he" leads him to the marlin (27-32). But he has profound contempt for the man-of-war jellyfish, which floated cheerfully "as a bubble with its long deadly purple filaments trailing a yard behind it in the water."

"'Agua mala', the man said, 'you whore'" (29).

Santiago thinks of the jellyfish as a woman even though he does not know its gender. His prejudices against women make themselves manifest at once. The tiny fish that swam between the filaments made themselves manifest at once. The tiny fish that swam between the filaments were immune to the poison of the jellyfish but men were not. The poisoning of the jellyfish "came quickly and struck like whiplash". Santiago's hatred of the Portuguese man-of-war which he associates with beautiful and poisonous women is expressed in the following passage:

> The iridescent bubbles were beautiful. But they were the falsest thing in the sea and the old man loved to see the big sea turtles eating them. The turtles saw them, approached them from the front, then shut their eyes so they were completely carapaced and ate them filaments and all. The old man loved to see the turtles eat them and he loved to walk on them on the beach after a storm and hear them pop when he stepped on them with the horny soles of his feet. (30)

This biased attitude recurs when he hooks the great marlin. He jumps to the conclusion that it is a male marlin. "But what a great fish *he* is and what *he* will bring in the market if the flesh is good. *He took the bait like a male and he pulls like a male and his fight has no panic in it*" (41). His belief that the female of the species gets panicky and that the male is always courageous and calm is reflected in his memory of how he had once hooked a female marlin, which made "a wild, panic-stricken, despairing fight that soon exhausted her". The nobility of the male is demonstrated by his allowing the female to feed first and, when the female is killed and hoisted aboard, staying by the side of the boat and jumping up high in the air beside the boat to see where his mate was. In Santiago's imagination, the male is calm, courageous, dignified and loving while the female is nervous and panicky (41-42). The female is painted in a poor light while the male is presented in bright colours.

This gender bias in Santiago's perception is carried forward to his attitude to the sea:

> He always thought of the sea as *la mar* which is what people call her in Spanish when they love her. Sometimes, those who love her say bad things of her but they are always said as though she were a woman.... But the old man always thought of her as feminine and as something that gave or withheld great favours, and if she did wild or wicked things it was because she could not help them. The moon affects her as it does a woman, he thought. (23-24)

Those who love the sea say bad things about her as though she were a woman. It is implied that bad things are associated with woman/the sea. He denigrates woman/the sea on two counts: (1) as dependent on the moon like a mentally unsound person (a lunatic), and (2) as a creature who does wild and wicked things like a demon or an evil spirit.

From a feminist point of view, Santiago is guilty of gender bias, but from a common sense point of view he is entitled to have his own views. He is free to think of woman/the sea as dependent on the moon or doing wild and wicked things. He has the freedom to put away his wife's photo out of sight in a corner and to call the Portuguese man-of-war "a whore". But such attitudes and actions make him the target of feminist critics like Martin Swan who find fault with him for misogyny.

Santiago shares his very masculine creator's prejudices which are common traditional views of mankind.

We learn a lot about Santiago from a few key sentences in the opening paragraphs of the novelette:

1. He was an old man who fished alone in a skiff in the Gulf Stream....
2. ...and he had gone eighty-four days now without taking a fish.
3. But after forty days without a fish the boy's parents had told him that the old man was now definitely and finally *salao*, which is the worst form of unlucky.

4. The old man was thin and gaunt with deep wrinkles in the back of his neck.
5. The brown blotches of the benevolent skin cancer the sun brings from its reflection on the tropic sea were on his cheeks.
6. The blotches ran well down the sides of his face and his hands had the deep-creased scars from handling heavy fish on the cords.
7. Everything about him was old except his eyes and they were the same colour as the sea and were cheerful and undefeated.
8. They sat on the terrace and many of the fishermen made fun of the old man and he was not angry.
9. He was too simple to wonder when he had attained humility. But he knew he had attained it and he knew it was not disgraceful and it carried no loss of true pride.
10. I am a strange old man.

The above sentences, which appear in the first six pages of the novel, not only describe the physical appearance of Santiago but also reveal his character and, to some extent, the qualities of his head and heart. Let us look at these key sentences one by one:

1. **"He was an old man who fished alone in a skiff in the Gulf Stream..."**

Santiago was an old fisherman. But he was not like other fishermen. He fished alone in the Gulf Stream. When we are told that he fished in a skiff (a small boat meant for a single person), we form the impression that he caught small fish; but we hasten to correct this impression later when we are told in the sixth key sentence cited above that "his hands had the deep-creased scars from handling heavy fish on the cords". We now learn that he was in the habit of catching heavy fish single-handedly rowing a small skiff. This explains the second key sentence.

2. **"...and he had gone eighty-four days now without taking a fish."**

Even an untrained fisherman, a novice, could easily have caught a few fish each day for there are innumerable small fish moving in schools in the sea and it would be a child's play to catch a few. But Santiago went without catching a single fish—not for one or two days—but for eighty-four days. How did he, a veteran fisherman, fail to catch some of those fishes which were falling into his lap? Besides, he had a boy with him the first forty days. The boy could surely have helped him catch some fish, or the boy himself could have caught a few small fish.

It becomes clear now that the old man refused to catch small fish. He had handled heavy fish in the past and, as we are told later on in the novel, he now wanted to catch the biggest fish of his life. He wanted to excel in his occupation and hence he chose to go without taking a fish for eighty-four days. He wanted to catch either a very big fish or no fish at all, for he took his occupation as a challenge and wanted to prove himself as the best fisherman. He would not be satisfied with catching any small fish as a professional necessity. He did not even bother about what people thought of him and did not relent when the boy's parents withdrew him from Santiago's boat, though he missed the boy, whom he loved much, now and then.

3. **"But after forty days without a fish the boy's parents had told him that the old man was now definitely and finally *salao*, which is the worst form of unlucky."**

People, in general, can not appreciate inspired geniuses, who set their sights very high and are not tempted by small allurements or rewards. They do not look normal to the world in general and are dismissed as 'eccentric' or 'unlucky' or 'useless' or as 'failures in life.' The boy's parents took the same view of Santiago. They concluded that he was *salao* or extremely unlucky, and associating with such a man would bring bad luck.

Santiago did not think much of luck. He knew that he was born to catch fish and he wanted to excel as a fisherman.

He responded to the call of his destiny and adventure and was determined to prove himself as a good fisherman by catching the biggest ever fish. His calling or duty was what mattered most to him and if some people considered him unlucky, it was their problem, not his.

4. Was he a strong and powerfully built man? No. He was "**thin and gaunt with deep wrinkles in the back of neck.**"

He was a thin athletic man without any fat in his body and the deep wrinkles in the back of his neck were probably caused by the weight of the line across his shoulders as he handled heavy fish.

5. He worked far out in the sea where his exposure to the hot tropical sun was maximum. Exposure of this kind to the merciless tropical sun led to brown blotches on his cheeks. "The brown blotches of the benevolent skin cancer the sun brings from its reflection on the tropic sea were on his cheeks." This skin cancer and these brown blotches speak volumes about his experiences and adventures as a veteran fisherman on the Gulf Stream, who did not keep close to the shore, like others of his occupation, but chose to go far out where nobody could help him and where he was alone, braving the scorching sun and the hazards of the sea to battle against the big, heavy fish. Santiago was a heroic fisherman, not just another fishermen who lived by fishing close to the shore.

6. The brown blotches, caused by his exposure to the sun on the high sea, ran down his cheeks and **"his hands were scarred by handling heavy fish on the cords".** These scars were the marks of his heroism. He was like a battle-scarred veteran of the seas.

We are told here in unmistakable terms that Santiago had handled heavy fish before his present dry spell of eighty-four days of no fish, and we also know the reason for the dry spell. It was not for want of fish but because of his reluctance to catch any but the biggest ever fish that he went without taking any fish for eighty-four days. But Santiago was not only gaunt but also taciturn and never explained to fellow fishermen why he had such a long dry spell. A hero does not explain or justify his failures, but presses forward until he achieves victory and proves his mettle. A hero is always cheerful inspite of his failures because he has faith in himself and his commitment. He never accepts defeat.

7. **"Everything about him was old except his eyes and they were the same colour as the sea and were cheerful and undefeated."**

The eyes reveal the spirit of a person. They are the windows through which the soul or spirit of a person shines like a lamp. Santiago had young eyes in an old body. They were the same colour as the sea, which is perpetually and eternally young, and revealed an unconquerable spirit. Santiago says after killing the Mako Shark: "'But man is not made for defeat', he said, 'A man can be destroyed but not defeated'." He was sad and depressed as the great marlin was mutilated by the Mako shark, who took about forty pounds of the marlin, and his harpoon and all the rope into the bargain; but he tried to cheer himself up into his original, happy cast of mind: "'Think about something cheerful, old man', he said, 'Every minute now you are closer to home you sail lighter for the loss of forty pounds.'"

8. **"They sat on the terrace and many of the fishermen made fun of the old man and he was not angry."**

We have already noted that Santiago was a cheerful, old man who had no bitterness at all about him. This is made amply clear by his affection for Manolin, the boy, who was several decades younger than he. At the terrace there were many successful fishermen who had caught sharks and other fish. Some fishermen made fun of Santiago, obviously because he was not catching any fish for days together, but he never lost his temper for he was a strange old man, aware of his inner strength and peace and had only love for others. Some old fishermen were more sympathetic, having grown mature with experience. The boy had gone fishing with the old man since he was five and became a great admirer of him. Hence "the old man looked at him with his sun-burned, confident loving eyes" (8), but he never felt superior or patronizing or parental about the boy for whom he had only warm, friendly feelings.

9. 'Humility' and 'love' are the two great qualities in human life worth achieving and the old man achieved them. When one does not have an 'ego problem' one learns to love truly and becomes capable of compassion and the higher kind of love known as 'agape' which is universal in character. **"He was too simple to wonder when he had attained humility. But he knew he had attained it and he knew it was not disgraceful and it carried no loss of true pride"** (9).

In other words he was humble but self-contained and strong. He was proud of himself as a fisherman but did not wear it on his sleeve.

10. Therefore, he believed that he was a strange old man. When Manolin points out that he (Santiago) went turtling for years but his eyes are good, even though it is generally believed that turtling hurts the eyes, he answers, **"I am a strange old man"** (10).

The novel, *The Old Man and the Sea*, is about this strange old fisherman called Santiago. Not only did he make the statement, cited above, to Manolin but, on the second day of his contest with the Marlin, he reminded himself of it: "'I told the boy I was a strange old man', he said, 'now so when I must prove it.'" This self-reminder during his struggle with the marlin sounds as if he had made a declaration about himself and he now had a responsibility to justify it. It also suggests that he had never got a chance to prove it earlier and got it only now. But the omniscient narrator who knows everything about Santiago informs us that the old man had proved it several times before:

> The thousand times that he had proved it meant nothing. Now he was proving it again. Each time was a new time and he never thought about the past when he was doing it. (58)

Achievers, in general, and creative artists, in particular, prove themselves again and again and, every time, it is a new experience and a new achievement.

Two very important questions trouble us here.

1. Did Santiago bring the mutilated fish to the shore, as an exhibition item, to show off his heroic achievement? Or, did he act in a natural way as an honest fisherman?
2. Could he have avoided shedding the marlin's blood in the sea, which attracted the sharks, by harpooning it? What other methods were open to him?

Let us proceed to scrutinize these questions.

We have formed a broad impression of Santiago's character from the opening paragraphs. Santiago does not strike us as a show man. He gives the impression of a normal, natural fisherman distinguished from the others by his vision and ambition, his heroic endeavor and endurance, and above all his indefatigable faith in himself.

If he was a showman, he would have brought in a large number of fish each day instead of going without a single fish for eighty-four days, or, he would have bragged about his ambition to catch the biggest ever fish and expressed his disdain for the simple satisfaction of catching small fish. If he caught a large number of fish everyday, he might have made up in quantity and number for his failure in showing quality. If he bragged about his ambition and priority, he would have negated the impression the omniscient narrator has given us that Santiago was a humble and simple fisherman.

A NOTE ON SANTIAGO'S HEROISM

Santiago's heroism is a blend of the old and the new. In him, we find the epic hero fighting valiantly a powerful adversary and overcoming him as well as a Christian hero treating his adversary as his brother and filled with love for him. We find in him a kind of David of the Old Testament fighting a Goliath in the form of a giant marlin. David went forth with the conviction that the Lord would deliver the giant into his hands even as Santiago had the faith that the Lord would deliver "a big one" into his hands. Later when the marlin took the bait he thought, "This far out he must be huge in this month" and again "he knew what a huge fish this was..." (35-36). At the height of the fight Santiago prayed to Jesus and Virgin Mary and made a vow to *Virgin de Cobre*. He prayed for the death of the 'wonderful' fish.

Later, we find that Santiago admired and loved the marlin, his adversary, to the point of saying, "I do not care who kills who" (82). He called the marlin his brother. He exhibits love, charity and compassion—virtues extolled in the New Testament.

In valour and courage, Santiago reminds us of Old Testament heroes like David and Samson, and in his love, endurance and compassion, he reminds us of Jesus and the Christian saints, who are also heroes in a different and higher sense.

SANTIAGO AND THE MARLIN

Did he have a choice in the manner of killing the marlin? If it were a young marlin smaller than his skiff, he might have struggled against it for a day or two more until it succumbed out of sheer exhaustion or he might have clubbed it to death. But it was a huge, oversized marlin two feet longer than his skiff and over 1500 pounds in weight, and it was impossible for him to haul it over into the skiff even if, for some reason or the other, the fish succumbed to death. If he somehow managed to land it in the skiff he would not be able to row it and would have been forced to swim alongside the skiff until he drowned and died or fell a prey to sharks and other powerful creatures in the sea.

Therefore, it stands to reason that the only course left to Santiago was to harpoon it causing bloodshed and attracting the sharks, the alternative being another day, the eighty-fifth day, of catching no fish. But the marlin caught the bait and was hooked, becoming inseparably linked with Santiago leaving him no alternative but to fight the marlin and vanquish it or get killed in the process.

But there was a time when he killed a marlin by clubbing her on the head. Santiago recalls the episode which made him and the boy sad for he played the cruel villain in the love-story of a marlin couple.

> ...The male fish always let the female fish feed first, and the hooked fish, the female, made a wild, panic-stricken, despairing fight that soon exhausted her, and all the time the male had stayed with her, crossing the line and circling with her on the surface.... When the old man had gaffed her and clubbed her, holding the rapier bill with its sandpaper edge and clubbing her across the top of her head until her colour turned to a colour almost like the backing of mirrors, and then, with the boy's aid, hoisted her aboard, the male fish had stayed by the side of the boat. Then, while the old man was clearing the lines and preparing the harpoon, the male fish jumped high in the air beside the boat to see where the female was and then went down deep,.... (42)

This episode is described in sentimental terms. It is reminiscent of sage Valmiki's sadness when he saw a fowler killing one of a pair of mating birds. Out of that sadness was born the first verse which inspired the great sage to write the great Sanskrit epic, *The Ramayana*. It would be unfair to call Santiago a sentimentalist as Gerry Brenner does in his excellent study, *The Old Man and the Sea*: *Story of a Common Man* (50), even as it would be in bad taste to call Valmiki a sentimentalist. Brener defines "sentimentalist as someone who assigns unwarranted or excessive emotions to people, creatures, or objects" (50). He faults Santiago for interpreting "the mating habits of the marlin as if they were like humans or, better, like geese, who mate for life" (51). He quotes Professor David Grobecker, director of the Pacific Game Fish Research Foundation in Kona, Hawaii, for scientific support to say that marlin do not mate for life. Brenner goes on to say: "Professor Grobecker acknowledges it is likely that the so-called mate of Santiago's hooked female may be a female marlin that follows the hooked female out of curiosity, circles out of perplexity at the hooked female's odd behaviour, and leaps out of water in puzzlement, not grief or farewell" (51).

Uncharitable critics might charge both Valmiki and Santiago with maudlin sentiment, but we should remember that 'fellow-feeling' is common to human beings, animals and birds.

Fellow-feeling springs out of the basic emotion that what happens to one member of the community might happen to another at some other time. This is a strange mixture of the emotions of curiosity and fear. Therefore, we need not be so uncharitable as to accuse the writer or the character of sentimentality or showing excess emotion.

Valmiki might not be aware of the mating habits of birds even as Santiago might not know enough about the mating habits of marlin. Whether it is a male that stayed with the hunted marlin or another female, the response would be about the same. The feeling of "every man's death diminishes me/for I am involved in mankind", as John Donne writes in one of his Devotions, is a basic human feeling on such occasions. One may call it 'curiosity' if one likes but it is an active, anxious 'curiosity' caused by empathy rather than an idle curiosity. The anxious feeling of 'what is happening to my fellow-creature now, may happen to me later, might have caused the marlin to jump up and see the dead marlin in the boat.'

Gerry Brenner questions Santiago's claim of strangeness and profession of love for the marlin: and underlines the fact that he is just a common man, not a sage old man:

> Yet if he has such tender feelings toward these noble marlin, why does he continue to fish for them? Why doesn't he fish for smaller fry, for quantities of tuna or dolphin or porpoise or whatever else brings a good price at market, rather than for a day's single big fish?...
>
> By anthropomorphizing the marlin of both the flashback and the central story, Santiago shows his inability to come to terms with his identity as killer and his need to continually apologize to creatures to whom he feels compelled to attribute human traits. At the least he is a mixed-up human being, not a sage old man. (50)

The very fact that he assigns human traits to the marlin and the other denizens of the sea and entertains tender feelings towards them marks him out as a strange old man. He feels sorry for the flying fish and the birds who have no chance against 'the one single lasting thing—the stream'. In the same way he feels sorry for the marlin but seems to be unaware that he has no chance either—which is a general delusion into which everybody falls—until the sharks strike. But then, even though he is rudely disillusioned, he fights like a hero without admitting defeat and his bravery and endurance mark him out as a strange old man.

Santiago fights like the heroes of yore who killed their foes in battle and dragged their corpses, lashed to their chariots, as Achilles did with Hector's corpse in *Iliad*.

He fought a losing battle bravely unwilling to surrender like Arjuna of Mahabharata fighting with Lord Siva in a hunter's form. Arjuna loses all the arrows of his inexhaustible quiver and fights with his bow. When he loses it, he fights with his bare hands until the great God is pleased with him, appears in his true divine form, and grants him boons.

Santiago loses his harpoon to the *dentuso* and his knife, gaff, oars, tiller and the short club to the galanos but still there is fight left in him.

The epic hero, Arjuna, brings home boons and divine weapons after his fight with Lord Siva; but Santiago's prize is the skeleton of the marlin and his boon is humility which is expressed by his remark to Manolin. "'They beat me, Manolin', he said, 'They truly beat me'." By 'they' he meant the sharks.

Earlier he had felt a coppery taste in his mouth making him afraid for a moment, and spat into the ocean (obviously blood). The omniscient narrator tells us at this juncture, "He knew he was beaten now finally and without remedy..." (107). The champion who had once beaten the powerful Negro in the hand game and who had won in the contest against the great marlin, was finally humbled by the sharks. The proud fisherman who said during his struggle with the marlin that a man could be destroyed but not defeated, finally admitted defeat to himself as well as to the boy. This ironic boon of humility, which makes him a sage old man, was granted to him by the inexorable forces of life and fate. Even the mightiest are humbled by these two powerful forces.

In *The Old Man and the Sea* they operate through the Gulf Stream against the backdrop of which the little drama of Santiago's struggles is enacted.

It may be said that Santiago acted wrongly and unethically in not releasing the marlin after killing it, instead of lashing it to the skiff and trying to take it home as a trophy, when he respected and loved it so much. He was born to be a fisherman and it was his duty to kill fish but, sometimes he saw a noble fish whom he respected but he had to kill it to fulfill his life as a fisherman.

When Arjuna saw his kith and kin and elders, whom he loved and respected, ranged against him in the Kurukshetra battlefield, in the *Mahabharata*, he did not find it in his heart to fight and kill them, and wanted to leave the battlefield. Lord Krishna, his chariot driver, taught him that he was born to fight and kill and should not chicken out and run away or feel sentimental and lay down his arms. There are many occasions in the war, when a hero admired or respected or loved an adversary, but had to fight against him and kill him. In *Ramayana*, when Rama and Ravana face each other, each admires the other but they fight a terrible battle in which Rama kills Ravana.

Santiago loves and respects the noble marlin, whom he calls his brother and enemy at once, and is forced to kill it as a fisherman. There is nothing unprofessional or unethical here as he acts like an honest, fearless and tough fisherman with tender human feelings. This is very much in keeping with the *New Yorker* portrait of Hemingway's brawny, hairy arm holding a rose.

Santiago conducts himself in the true epic tradition and his act in lashing the carcass of the marlin should not be misconstrued as "a self-glorifying power trip", in the words of Gerry Brenner (56).

SANTIAGO'S DREAMS AND DAYDREAMS

One of the recurring dreams and daydreams of Santiago is about the lions playing on the beach. His memory of standing on the deck of a ship and seeing the lions on the African beach is the source of these dreams. Another source of his daydreams is his memory of the great baseball hero, DiMaggio. Both are regal images—one in the animal world and the other in the sports world. These daydreams indicate Santiago's ambition to excel as a fisherman and underline his strangeness. Why does he not dream of other lesser animals like monkeys, foxes or rabbits? He wants to draw strength and determination, to recharge his batteries by thinking of the lions. In the same way his daydreams of DiMaggio help him to draw fresh inspiration and energy, and measure himself up against a great player.

He identifies himself with the king of the jungle and the king of baseball, and these two images form part of his reserve energies from which he draws in times of need and exhaustion.

There are other images, which are born out of his memories and his life on the shore—one is the image of himself as a champion in the handgame and the other is the image of Manolin, his alter-ego, who serves as the boy in himself calling up his youthful energy to assist him.

The images of the king of the jungle and the king of baseball and the image of himself as a champion in the handgame emerging from his memory all underline his ambitions to prove himself the king of fishermen. This self-test and achievement is not meant for publicity or fame or money but only for self-satisfaction and self-fulfillment.

Santiago does not dream of his wife who is no more. He does not dream of women nor storms nor of great fish nor fights nor contests of strength, he only dreams of places and the lions on the beach.

His wife died a long time ago and there was once an old tinted photograph of her on the wall but it made him lonely and he took it down and put it on the shelf in the corner under his shirt.

It is natural for many old people to dream of places and not to have erotic or exotic dreams involving actions and happenings. But he still thinks of himself as a good fisherman and is in love with the sea and its denizens; but, as he is very old, he takes the help of his memories and dreams of symbols of power like the lions, the great baseball player, DiMaggio and the boy. But he does not dream of the boy as the boy meets him every day and, in fact, is part of his mental make-up. The boy is the tyro and the old man the tutor. The boy is like the old man's own son. Even though the old man cannot exercise paternal authority over him, the boy is an image and inspiration which he leans on. Besides, the boy is always in his mind and makes him wish for his (the boy's) presence. He misses Manolin physically but still draws energy from the thought of him.

SANTIAGO AND MANOLIN

The relationship between the old man and the boy is a tender, beautiful aspect of the novel—the guru and his disciple, the foster father and his adopted son, the veteran fisherman and his young assistant, deep friendship between an old man and a young boy—dealing with mutual love between Santiago and Manolin, the former's gentle love and affection for the boy, and the latter's love and admiration for the old man. When they converse they are like two friends of about the same age with common interests. They talk about fishing and baseball. They are both great admirers of DiMaggio, Dick Sisler and John J. Mcgrow as individual players and the Yankees as a team.

When it comes to fishing, the boy thinks that Santiago is the best fisherman.

From the text of the novel, it is clear that the boy represents the world outside to the old man. Santiago is not shown talking with anybody except the boy and, when the boy is not present, he talks to himself or to the fish or to the birds. The boy is not only a source of energy to the old man but his connection with the world—in short, his world. Hence, if he has to prove something it is to the boy. Like a stage artiste performing for his audience, Santiago performs for the boy and, in a way, for the boy within himself. That is why he says during the height of the struggle with the marlin: "'I told the boy I was a strange old man', he said, 'Now is when I must prove it.'" It is enough if he proves it to Manolin. It is as good as proving it to the world.

Like a friend, the boy offers beer to the old man, engages him in a dialogue on baseball, in which both are passionately interested, participates in the daily fiction of a pot of yellow rice and the cast net.

Manolin is like Santiago's adopted son and pupil learning from him and assisting him in the boat from the age of five. He is like a loving mother or wife taking care of the old man in everyway: "When the old man sleeps in the chair he covers him with a blanket, goes out and comes back with supper. When the old man refuses to eat, he cajoles him into eating. He has brought black beans and rice, fried bananas, and some stew and two beer bottles from the Terrace."

Manolin is so thoughtful for the old man that he plans to get water for him, as the village water supply is two streets down the road, and provide him with a soap, a good towel, a shirt and a jacket for winter, new shoes and another blanket.

Like a young son looking upon his father as the greatest man in the world or a young student regarding his teacher as a role model or a hero, Manolin looks upon Santiago as the greatest fisherman in the world. After such adoration, Santiago has a compulsive need to prove himself equal to any challenge on the sea, and proving it to the boy, who thinks the world of him, is as good as proving it to the whole world and winning the 'Nobel Prize for fishing', if there were such a prize. The boy's company boosts Santiago's ego and fills him with energy. Hence in times of exhaustion and desperation, the old man wishes for the boy's presence.

Once the old man is on the sea, he is alone with it and its denizens and with himself. He speaks to all three. But after he returns to the shore, the boy is with him again helping him and taking care of him. The beaten or tired old man sleeps face down with the palms of his hands up. The boy comes in the morning as usual and sees the old man's hands and cries. Then he goes out and brings hot coffee and waits for the old man. Santiago sleeps for a long time and the boy heats the coffee again. He does not disturb the old man. Then he wakes up, and the boy gives him coffee. The old man tells him that he was beaten, but the boy puts it in perspective by saying that he was not beaten by the marlin and the old man agrees and says that he was beaten later meaning that he was beaten by an overwhelming number of *galano* sharks.

Then the boy is entrusted with the task of giving away the remains of the marlin by the old man—the head for Pedrico who is looking after the skiff and the gear, and the spear for the boy himself. The old man wants a good killing lance and a new knife, and the boy undertakes to procure them for the next fishing trip of the old man. Then he brings a clean shirt, food, newspapers and some balm for the hands of the old man. He cries as he goes out at the sad condition of the old man. When he returns the old man is still asleep and the boy sits by his side and watches.

Thus Manolin cares for and nurses the old man with loving affection.

How old is Manolin? Is he a boy or a teenager? Santiago always refers to him as the boy even though he calls him 'a man' in banter: "'you bought me a beer', the old man said, 'you are already a man'" (8) the dialogue between Santiago and Manolin before the old man sets out on his adventure is not only interesting but also significant in that it establishes the importance of the boy for the old man, for the boy is part of the old man's mental make-up.

During their discussion of the great baseball players, DiMaggio and Dick Sisler, Manolin says: "The great Sisler's father was never poor and he, the father, was playing in the big leagues when he was my age."

C. Harold Hurley throws interesting light on how Hemingway manipulates the third-person pronoun 'he' to differentiate between 'the great Sisler's father' and 'the great Sisler'.

> In the first instance—"he, the father"—the pronoun "he", qualified by "the father", refers obviously, to "the great Sisler's father" conversely, in the second instance—

> "when he was my age"—the unqualified "he" refers, less obviously, to "the great Sisler", the focus of Santiago and Manolin's exchange. (71-72)

Now we know that the great Sisler was Manolin's age when his father, George Sisler was playing in the major leagues, and this helps us in arriving at an idea of Manolin's age. Hurley offers this explanation in this context:

> When the elder Sisler retired from baseball in 1930, his son Dick, born a decade earlier, was a ten-year-old boy. In that George did not play beyond his son's tenth birth day, and in that Dick Sisler was Manolin's age when George was playing in the major leagues, Manolin himself can be no more than ten years old. (72)

But Manolin is mature beyond his years. He is mentally prepared and eager to go against his parents' orders in order to learn everything, not just fishing, from Santiago, who is his friend, philosopher and guide. If Santiago wants to teach him what a man can do, Manolin wants to learn from him what a man must do. If Santiago is the tutor, Manolin is the tyro.

Santiago's being a fisherman and his strange power over Manolin as a tutor figure puts us in mind of the fisherman image in the *New Testament* and the greatest fisherman of them all, Jesus:

> And Jesus, walking by the sea of Galilee, saw two brethren, Simon called Peter, and Andrew his brother, casting a net into the sea: for they were fishers.
>
> And he saith unto them, follow me, and I will make you fishers of men.
>
> And, they straightway left their nets, and followed him.
>
> And going on from thence, he saw other two brethren, James the son of Zebedee, and John his brother, in a ship with Zebedee their father, mending their nets; and he called them.
>
> And they immediately left the ship and their father, and followed him. (St. Matthew, 4:18-22)

Manolin said to Santiago, "And the best fisherman is you" and again "'Que va', the boy said, 'there are many good fishermen and some great ones. But there is only you'" (17-18).

Manolin wanted to go with Santiago but his father made him leave the old man.

Towards the end of the novel, Manolin declares his resolve to leave his father and follow Santiago.

> 'Now we fish together again.'
> 'No. I am not lucky. I am not lucky anymore.'
> 'The hell with luck', the boy said, 'I'll bring the luck with me.'
> 'What will your family say?'
> 'I do not care. I caught two yesterday. But we will fish together now for I still have much to learn.' (112-113)

Manolin decided to leave his father and follow Santiago even as James and John left their father, Zebedee, and followed Jesus. He believed that he would learn everything including fishing from Santiago even as Simon, Andrew, James and John learnt everything including the fishing of men from Jesus.

THE MARLIN

If we look upon Santiago as the hero of the novel, the adversary is the marlin. He seems to have a tryst with the marlin far out in the sea, for when he parts with Manolin and rows out of the harbour the author tells us that the other fishermen spread apart after they were out of the mouth of the harbour and each one headed for the part of the ocean where he hoped to find fish. "The old man knew he was going far out and he left the smell of the land behind and rowed out into the clean early morning smell of the ocean" (22). He was going far out because he wanted to find the marlin like Theseus finding the Minotaur who stayed far out in the deep dark labyrinth in Greek mythology.

When Santiago finally hooks the marlin, he says:

> His choice had been to stay in the deep dark water far out beyond all snares and traps and treacheries. My

> choice was to go there to find him beyond all people. Beyond all people in the world. Now we are joined together and have been since noon. And no one to help either one of us. (43)

The marlin stayed in the deep dark water and the old man did not know that it was a marlin eating the sardines that covered the hook one hundred fathoms down.

He did not know what kind of fish it was. But he felt that something was eating the sardines carefully avoiding the hook from the gentle pull on the line. He gave more line and when the fish ate the tuna and got the hook in the mouth, he felt a stronger pull. He released more line as the weight increased.

The fish was hooked at noon and at sunset the old man still had no knowledge what kind of fish it was. The hooked fish was pulling the boat powerfully towards the north-west. For a moment Santiago was afraid that the fish might dive down. But the unknown fish continued to pull the boat. The old man wished for the boy repeatedly as he was struggling against the unseen and unknown adversary, who was towing his boat: "I wish I could see him. I wish I could see him only once to know what I have against me" (39). Now the boat was moving away from the distant glow of Havana eastwards. During the night two porpoises—a blowing male and a sighing female came around the boat. All the while the fish was pulling the boat powerfully and Santiago found him wonderful and strange.

> Never have I had such a strong fish nor one who acted so strangely. Perhaps he is too wise to jump. He could ruin me by jumping or by wild rush. But perhaps he has been hooked many times before and he knows that this is how he should make his fight. He cannot know that it is only one man against him, nor that it is an old man. But what a great fish he is and what he will bring in the market if the flesh is good. He took the bait like a male and he pulls like a male and his fight has no panic in it. (41)

Thus Santiago admires the marlin, before knowing that it is a marlin, and develops a respect for him. Then he remembered the sad episode of the marlin couple, how he hooked, killed and hoisted the female aboard, and how the male, who had stayed by the side of the boat all the while, jumped up high into the air to see where the female was. Santiago and the boy, who was then with him, felt very sad for the marlin couple. This memory made the old man wish for the boy repeatedly and feel a personal relationship with the fish. It roused a special feeling in the old man's heart for the great fish he had hooked. This is expressed in sentences like "'Fish', he said, 'I love you and respect you very much. But I will kill you dead before this day ends'", (46) and "I wish I could feed the fish, he thought. He is my brother", and "never have I seen a greater, or more beautiful, or a calmer or more noble thing than you, brother...and ...I have killed this fish which is my brother and now I must do the slave work" (51, 82, 84-85).

The marlin gave a good fight—a fight which the old man would remember the rest of his life. The marlin suffered great physical agony with the hook in his mouth but he made the old man suffer as much causing a cramp in his hand, pulling him overboard, towing the boat farther and farther away using his more than fifteen hundred pounds of weight—causing the taut line to cut his palms and shoulders.

He saw nearly the whole fish when it came up for a while and this is what he saw:

> The line rose slowly and steadily and then the surface of the ocean bulged ahead of the boat and the fish came out. He came out unendingly and water poured from his sides. He was bright in the sun and his head and back were dark purple. And in the sun the stripes on his sides showed wide and a light lavender. His sword was as long as a baseball bat and tapered like a rapier and he rose his full length from the water and then re-entered it, smoothly, like a diver and the old man saw the great scythe blade of his tail go under and the line commenced to race out. (54)

Now Santiago understood that it was a huge marlin two feet longer than the skiff and weighing more than a thousand and five hundred pounds. Santiago attributes human qualities like dignity, greatness, brotherliness, strangeness and strength and power to the fish. This adds an extra dimension to the fish and the fisherman and their relationship. The handgame between him and the big Negro serves as a dramatic correlative for the life-and-death tug-of-war between the marlin and the old man. When he finally won in the combat, it was not before he was thrown down in the boat and getting hurt a few times. Like the old man, we are also filled with admiration for the noble fish who endured great pain and gave a good fight to his enemy-cum-brother for nearly three days. In this respect, he was like Santiago who also endured great pain for three days fighting the marlin first and the sharks later, and finally prevailed. Hence the old man saw something of himself in the marlin and called him his brother. Both shared the admirable qualities of strangeness, endurance and a certain kind of bravery, dignity and nobility. The marlin may be called the Santiago of the sea who fights a lonely battle with his worthy adversary. In a certain respect he is greater than Santiago who took his nourishment eating a tuna and a bonita and a dolphin, but the marlin had nothing to eat and, with the cruel hook in his mouth, had to go without food. But he fought bravely and, in the estimation of Santiago, his worth and dignity rose further.

> Then he was sorry for the great fish that had nothing to eat and his determination to kill him never relaxed in his sorrow for him. How many people will he feed, he thought. But are they worthy to eat him? No, of course not. There is no one worthy of eating him from the manner of his behaviour and his great dignity. (66)

The marlin's choice, like that of Melville's Moby Dick, was to stay in the deep dark water far out beyond all snares and traps and treacheries. Santiago's choice, like Ahab's, was to go there to find him beyond all people and challenge him to single combat like in medieval romances, where noble and dignified emotions and conduct mattered more than anything else.

Neither the marlin nor Santiago asked for the fight but Santiago was born to catch fish even as the marlin was born to feed on other fish in the sea, in accordance with the law of the sea.

After the hide-and-seek part of the preliminary combat during which they are linked together by the line and the hook, the marlin showed itself as a huge fish, sword and all, for a while, and the old man had a glimpse of the marlin and found that he was larger than the skiff and identified him as the biggest marlin he had ever seen.

Later, when the marlin was circling he passed under the boat and his length was incredibly great.

> But he was that big and at the end of his circle, he came to the surface only thirty yards away and the man saw his tail out of water. It was higher than a big scythe blade a very pale lavender above the dark blue water. It raked back and as the fish swam just below the surface the old man could see his huge bulk and the purple stripes that banded him. His dorsal fin was down and his huge pectorals were spread wide.
>
> On this circle the old man could see the fish's eye and the two grey sucking fish that swam around him. Sometimes they attached themselves to him. Sometimes they darted off. Sometimes they would swim easily in his shadow. They were each over three feet long and when they swam fast they lashed their whole bodies like eels. (80)

The above is a close-up view of the marlin as seen by Santiago when the fish passed under the boat. He was stunningly and unbelievably large and Santiago clearly saw his eye and the two sucking fish who attached themselves to him—each three-feet long.

Later on, just before his death the fish jumped up into the air giving the old man a full view of his whole body. It happened when Santiago drove his harpoon into the fish's side:

> Then the fish came alive, with his death in him, and rose high out of the water showing all his great length and width and all his power and his beauty. He seemed to hang in the air above the old man in the skiff. Then he fell into the water with a crash that sent spray over the old man and over all of the skiff. (84)

Thus, we, with the old man, have a full view of the great fish in what marks the climax of the combat between the old man and the marlin.

The great fish in the air presents a vision of power and glory. What follows is a gory vision of the fish on his back with his silver belly up and the sea turning red with the blood of his heart where the harpoon pierced him. The old man's heroic enthusiasm and joy of victory turned into pathos, grief and repentance when he laid his head on his hands and said: "I am a tired old man. But I have killed this fish which is my brother and now I must do the slave work" (84-85).

The old man's affinity with the marlin is expressed at different times in different words when he calls the fish his 'brother' and his 'friend' and identifies himself totally with the fish:

> You are killing me, fish, the old man thought. But you have a right to. Never have I seen a greater, or more beautiful, or a calmer or more noble thing than you, brother. Come on and kill me. I do not care who kills who. (82)

OTHER DENIZENS OF THE SEA: BIRDS AND BEASTS

Santiago is like Coleridge's ancient mariner who learns that love for all living creatures is the best prayer:

> He prayeth best who loveth best
> Both man and bird and beast.

He loves the flying fish and the birds and is full of compassion for them as the birds are very delicate and are always flying in vain:

> He was very fond of flying fish as they were his principal friends on the ocean. He was sorry for the birds, especially the small delicate dark terns that were always flying and looking and almost never finding, and he thought, 'The birds have a harder life than we do except for the robber birds and the heavy strong ones. Why did they make birds so delicate and fine as those sea swallows when the ocean can be so cruel? She is kind and very beautiful. But she can be so cruel and it comes so suddenly and such birds that fly, dipping and hunting, with their small sad voices are made too delicately for the sea.' (23)

He is sorry for the delicate terns and the sea swallows, who are too delicate for the sea that can be very cruel at times.

He, then, sees a man-of-war bird, with long black wings, circling in the sky, trying to catch the flying fish. He also sees a big school of dolphin chasing the flying fish. His vast experience tells him that the bird has no chance as the flying fish are too big for him and travel too fast, but the school of dolphin is too big and too widespread for the flying fish, and the flying fish have no chance.

After some time the bird circles above again and, a little later, a small tuna is seen and then another and yet another and a school of them and one of them is hooked and caught by the old man, who plans to use it as a bait. The boy has given him two tunas earlier and they are used as baits already. Santiago has four different baits at different depths—one at forty fathoms, the second at seventy-five fathoms, and the third and the fourth at one hundred and one hundred and twenty-five fathoms.

He tells himself to remember to eat the tuna in the morning in order to keep strong.

During the night two porpoises come, a male and a female—the male making a blowing noise and the female a sighing blow. The old man likes them as they play and make jokes and love one another. He calls them his brothers like the flying fish.

He remembers the sad episode of how he once hooked one of a pair of marlin, how the female made wild, panic-stricken struggles and was exhausted until she was killed and hauled into the boat, and how the male fish stayed with them all the time and jumped high into the air to have a last look at his mate.

Sometime before day-break an unknown fish takes one of the baits causing a little problem for the old man, locked in a life-and-death tug-of-war with the great marlin, who took the bait at a depth of one hundred fathoms. He does not want to lose the great marlin on account of the other nameless fish—a marlin or a broad bill or a shark. Hence he decides to get rid of it, and cuts it away.

There is a delightful interlude at this point, involving a small, warbling bird, providing the much needed relief and relaxation from tension. He is a small tired warbler flying over the boat and he flies around the old man's head and rests on the line a little more comfortably.

> 'How old are you?' the old man asked the bird. 'Is this your first trip?'
>
> The bird looked at him when he spoke. He was too tired even to examine the line and he teetered on it as his delicate feet gripped it fast.
>
> 'It's steady', the old man told him. 'It's too steady. You shouldn't be that tired after a windless night. What are birds coming to?'
>
> The hawks, he thought, that come out to sea to meet them. But he said nothing of this to the bird who could not understand him anyway and who would learn about the hawks soon enough.
>
> 'Take a good rest, small bird,' he said. 'Then go in and take your chance like any man or bird or fish.'
>
> It encouraged him to talk because his back had stiffened in the night and it hurt truly now.

> 'Stay at my house if you like, bird,' he said. 'I am sorry I can not hoist the sail and take you in with the small breeze that is rising. But I am with a friend. (48)

The little bird needs rest as the old man needs rest, as the great marlin needs rest, and as we, readers, caught in the tension of the fight between the old man and the marlin, need a little relief and relaxation before tension builds up again.

It is amusing to find the old man talking to the bird. He wonders why the bird is so tired after a windless night and what is wrong with birds these days. Then he remembers the danger to little birds from hawks. But he does not talk about it to the little bird as it would learn about the hawks soon.

Then he asks the bird to take rest for a while before going out and taking his chance like any man or bird or fish. The need for rest is uppermost in the old man's mind and after some time he is to snatch a little rest settling comfortably against the wood and taking his suffering and saying his prayers.

Santiago talks to the bird as if he were talking with a human being; he talks gently and kindly and lovingly as if the small bird were Manolin visiting him for a little while in a mysterious way. It is characteristic of the old man to adopt a gentle, kindly and loving attitude and tone while speaking to the birds and beasts of the sea as well as the boy.

THE SHARKS

The old man's struggles on the sea fall into two parts—his struggle with the great marlin and his struggles with the sharks, most of which take place in the night. An hour after he lashes the great fish to his boat, the first shark, a noble Mako shark, picks up the scent of blood and comes to the skiff. The old man sees it only when he breaks the surface of the water. He feels an admiration for this huge, powerful shark, who has no fear at all and would do exactly as he wishes:

> He was a very big Mako shark built to swim as fast as the fastest fish in the sea and everything about him was beautiful except his jaws: his back was as black as a

> sword fish's and his belly was silver and his hide was smooth and handsome. He was built as a sword fish except for his huge jaws which were tight shut now as he swam fast, just under the surface with his high dorsal fin knifing through the water without wavering. Inside the closed double lip of his jaws all of his eight rows of teeth were slanted inwards. They were not the ordinary pyramid-shaped teeth of most sharks. They were shaped like a man's fingers when they are crisped like claws. They were nearly as long as the fingers of the old man and they had razor sharp cutting edges on both sides. This was a fish built to feed on all the fishes in the sea, that were so fast and strong and well armed that they had no other enemy. (90)

The size and shape of the Mako shark are described in greater detail than those of the great marlin, which are left, for the most part, to our imagination. We are not informed about the jaws or teeth of the marlin. All that we know is that the fish is huge and powerful, and two feet longer than the skiff.

When the shark hits the marlin and rips off a big chunk of flesh, the old man drives his harpoon into the head of the fish between his eyes with all his strength and kills it. The dead shark goes down taking forty pounds of marlin's flesh and the harpoon and all the rope.

It is at this juncture that the old man tries autosuggestion talking to himself aloud, that man is not made for defeat and a man can be destroyed but not defeated. He pays tributes to the Mako shark: "The *dentuso* is cruel and able and strong and intelligent", (93) and a little later, "He lives on the live fish as you do. He is not a scavenger nor just a moving appetite as some sharks are. He is beautiful and noble and knows no fear of anything" (95).

Even as Santiago savours his encounter with the Mako shark and before he recovers from it, the Galanos strike. His instant response to the sight of the first of them is 'Ay'. "There is no translation for this word and perhaps it is just a noise such as a man might make, involuntarily, feeling the nail go through his hands and into the wood" (96).

The calvary allusion is obvious as is the connotation. The Galanos are like the Roman soldiers who crucified Jesus.

"They were hateful sharks, bad-smelling, scavengers as well as killers, and when they were hungry they would bite at an oar or the rudder of a boat" (97). They are cruel and brutal. The old man kills both of them who die chewing the great marlin's flesh. He has lashed his knife to the butt of one of the oars to kill them. Then comes another of them like a pig to the trough. The old man drives the knife on the oar into his brain. When the shark jerks backwards, the knife snaps.

The harpoon and the knife gone now, the old man has the gaff, the two oars, and the short club. He has some respite until sunset when a pack of Galanos attacks the marlin's carcass. He fought bravely and desperately using his club for some time. When the club is gone, he uses his tiller to fight the sharks until it breaks. Then he fights with the splintered butt until the last shark rolls away.

The Galanos are compared to pigs and wild dogs. Unlike the great marlin or the noble *dentuso*, they are cruel, and brutal monsters.

THE SEA

The sea is a powerful presence in *The Old Man and the Sea*. She is at once cruel and kind and beautiful. Santiago thinks of her as *la mar* as she is called in Spanish. People may say bad things about her but they are always said as though she were a woman. Some younger fishermen refer to her as *el mar*, which is masculine, and as a contestant or a place or an enemy. The old man thinks of her as one who gives or withholds great favours and, sometimes, does wild or wicked things because she cannot help them. She is affected by the moon like a woman.

Towards the end of the novel, the tired old man asks the boy if they searched for him. The boy says that they did with coastguard and planes. Then the old man comments, "The ocean is very big and a skiff is small and hard to see," (112) reminding us of the contrapuntal theme, which is central to all of Hemingway's works. Man, with all his claims of efforts and achievements is insignificant against the background of the everlasting things, represented by the Gulf Stream here. His so-called glories and achievements float insignificantly against "the one single lasting thing—the stream".

DIMAGGIO

A powerful recurring memory of the old man, besides that of the boy, is DiMaggio, the great baseball player. Santiago is a great admirer of DiMaggio, whose memory, like the boy's, supplies fresh energy to him in his struggles on the sea. He feels a special affinity with DiMaggio, whose father was a fisherman, and wishes to take the great player fishing. DiMaggio is his role model in his efforts to achieve excellence.

Therefore, he wants to do things perfectly so that DiMaggio may approve his performance:

> But I must have confidence and I must be worthy of the great DiMaggio who does all things perfectly even with the pain of the bone spur in his heel. (59)

Santiago does not know what a bone spur is, but knows that it must be a very painful condition. If DiMaggio has a bone spur, Santiago's hands and back hurt equally badly, and this gives him some satisfaction.

After killing the great marlin, the old man feels happy and thinks that the great DiMaggio would be proud of him.

THE TOURISTS AT THE TERRACE

Hemingway rounds off the novel, with his characteristic irony, describing a party of tourists at the Terrace. A woman in the party looks down in the water and sees the skeleton of the great marlin amid the empty beer cans and dead barracuda, itself an ironic circumstance, for we know what it is and how it came there, and were there with the old man watching the great three-day fight.

She asks a waiter what it is. "'Tiburon', the waiter said, 'Eshark.' He was meaning to explain what had happened" (114).

The woman understands that it is a shark; so does her male companion. But both admire the beautifully formed tail of the fish.

The ironic gap between the old man's great fight with the great marlin and the ignorance of the tourists, who represent the world outside, is strikingly comic.

The old man sleeps, blissfully ignorant of the tourists' ignorance. The party of tourists represent the normal flux of life which serves as a backdrop for the old man's dramatic fight with the marlin.

11

Critical Reception

Hemingway used to talk of "The Sea Book" as a trilogy. The "Bimini" and "Cuba" sections of *Islands in the Stream* were titled "The Sea When Young", and "The Sea When Absent" in the trilogy. Santiago's story was "The Sea in Being". "Bimini" was written in 1947, "Cuba" in December 1950, and the Santiago story after the 1950 Christmas holiday. Hemingway completed the Santiago story by the end of February 1951. In early March of 1951, he started writing another story that became the "At Sea" section of *Islands*. By Mid-May he had a tetralogy, in place of the projected trilogy, on his hands.

Some of his friends saw the typescript of the Santiago story and praised it. The word spread and *Cosmopolitan* offered to publish it for $10,000. Hemingway rejected the offer as he was mightily pleased with the story. He wrote to Charles Scribner: "This is the prose that I have been working for all my life that should read easily and simply and seem short and yet have all the dimensions of the visible world and the world of a man's spirit. It is as good prose as I can write as of now" (*Letters*, 738). By March 1952, he discarded the two titles that came to his mind—"The Sea in Being" and "The Dignity of Man". In May 1952, he agreed to have the story published in a single issue of *Life*, under the title "The Old Man and the Sea" for $21,000. The sales were gratifying. *Life* sold 53,00,000 copies of its September 1 issue and the first printing of the Book-of-the-Month club edition sold 1,53,000 copies. Scribner's edition reached the top of the bestseller lists and stayed there for half a year.

The critical reception of this novella resembles the undulating motions of the old man's skiff on the sea—generally favourable during the first decade of its publication and from mid 1960s rather mixed with the detractors outweighing the admirers but still widely read and regarded as the last significant work of Hemingway's lifetime, as a Pulitzer Prize winning novel, and as the immediate cause of the Nobel Prize. It won the Pulitzer Prize in 1952 and the American Academy of Arts and Letters Award of Merit Medal and contributed to Hemingway's selection for the 1954 Nobel Prize for Literature.

The Old Man and the Sea got a very good press. Most of the book reviews were very favourable. Edward Weeks paid a glowing tribute describing it as "Hemingway at His Best" (*Atlantic*, September 1952); Harvey Breit called it "a great and true novel, touching and terrible, tragic and happy" (*Nation*, September 6, 1952). Robert G. Davis praised the novel as "a tale superbly told", which implies "a human continuity that far transcends an individual relationship" (*New York Times Book Review*, September 7, 1952); Fanny Butcher extolled the book as an epic and "a great American classic of man's battle with a Titan of the sea" (*Chicago Sunday Tribune*, September 7, 1952); Joseph H. Jackson opined that it was "as perfect a piece of work as Hemingway has ever done" and described it as a "miracle-play of Man against Fate" (*San Francisco Chronicle*, September 7, 1952); Henry S. Canby thought it "the best fishing story in English" and praised Hemingway's narrative art: "Through Hemingway's matchless skill, a fishing story becomes a master piece" (*Book-of-the-Month Club News,* August 1952). The best tribute came from William Faulkner, Hemingway's contemporary and a great novelist who had already won the Nobel Prize for Literature. He found the novella to be Hemingway's best: "Time may show it to be the best single piece of any of us, I mean his and my contemporaries" (*Shenandoah*, Autumn 1952).

There were a few dissenting voices among the reviews. Orville Prescott found a lot of artificiality in Santiago's thoughts and that he was more a symbolic attitude than a man of flesh and blood (*New York Times,* August 28, 1952); Mark Schorer praises the fable-like virtues of the novella but finds fault with the authorial intrusions which mar the purity and lucidity of writing (*New Republic,* October 6, 1952); Delmore Schwartz commended the fishing narrative and the "vividness of presentation" but deprecated Hemingway's handling of Santiago's emotions (*Partisan Review*, November-December 1952).

Humanistic critics like Philip Young, Leo Gurko, and Clinton S. Burhans highly commended the novel. Philip Young, in his 1952 book on Hemingway, called the novella "an epic metaphor" and highly appreciated the story's "veneration for humanity, for what can be done and endured, and this grasp of man's kinship with the other creatures of the world, and with the world itself, is itself a victory of substantial proportions. It is the knowledge that a simple man is capable of such decency, dignity, and heroism, and that his struggle can be seen in heroic terms, that largely distinguishes this book" (100). According to Leo Gurko, Hemingway created "a hero whose triumph consists of searching his own powers to their absolute limits regardless of the physical results (14). Clinton S. Burhans sees a message in favour of team spirit, solidarity, and love as opposed to isolated individualism, in the symbols of DiMaggio, the pride of lions, and the Christological parallel (264).

Carlos Baker, a great admirer and discerning critic of Hemingway, finds Hemingway's 'ancient mariner' compassionate, courageous, and fraternal, but he emphasizes the work's symbolism, in general, and its Christian symbolism, in particular. He calls attention to Santiago's piety and suffering, and his experience as a form of martyrdom that made the novella a biblical parable. He sees a philosophical symbolism in it, with the Spanish Main symbolizing "that more extensive main, or main stream, where we all drift or sail, with or against the wind, in fair weather or foul, with our prize catches and our predatory sharks, and each of us, perhaps, like the ancient mariner of Coleridge, with some kind of albatross round his neck" (311).

Joseph Waldmeir interpreted the novella's religious symbols and numerology as part of an allegorical commentary of secularized religion e.g. the old man fishing with the boy for forty days and then fishing alone for forty-four days, struggling with the marlin for three days and landing him on the seventh attempt, killing the evil sharks and resting seven times (349-356).

Arvin S. Wells, acknowledging the Christological references in the novel and Santiago's humility, faith, and charity, concludes that his capacity for suffering transformed his ordeal into a religious mystery and that his identification with the marlin's "beauty, nobility, courage, calmness and endurance" redeemed his own "life from meaninglessness and futility" (97).

Earl Rovit finds a Jungian, archetypal motif of separation—initiation—return in Santiago's journey and in "his final rites of purification far out in the wilderness, beyond the glow of lights from Havana". Like all archetypal heroes, Santiago returns to his community bringing "back from his isolation a fragmented gift offering to his fellows, an imperfect symbol to suggest where he has been and what he found there" so that his community may benefit from his extraordinary experience (88-90).

Bickford Sylvester finds little interdependence between man and nature in the novella. He finds in the work a 'universal order', in which man's opposition to nature is paradoxically shown as necessary to vitality. According to him, Santiago's "compassionate violence" against the marlin shows that the "coincidence between the journey of the sun and the various rounds of combat implies consonance with an order which is supra-animate." He calls the novella's myth "profoundly humanistic", and sees in it "a modern parable of man's fallen state in which the universe requires man to overcome more in order to achieve what is necessary for all creatures" (132, 135, 136).

Wirt Williams regards the novel as the culmination of Hemingway's complex tragic vision (172-197).

Robert P. Weeks, in his introduction to the collection of critical essays on Hemingway, comments that, in *The Old Man and the Sea*, Hemingway confers on a seemingly routine experience affecting ordinary people a cosmic significance (*Critical Essays*, 15-16).

A decline in the critical graph can be seen in the same decade. The same Robert P. Weeks, who praised Hemingway in glowing terms, fulminates against Hemingway for filling *The Old Man and the Sea* with fakery, citing Santiago's claim that he could once "see quite well in the dark", that he could detect the marlin's gender and know of its nibbling on the bait at the end of a 600 ft. long line; and that he knows the signs of a coming hurricane, and the number of the teeth in the Mako shark [eight rows] (188-92).

But we should be a little charitable and make allowances for a simple fisherman's conjectures which need not be denounced as fakery.

Philip Young withdraws his earlier praise of the novella in 1966, objecting to its affectation of simplicity, its autobiographical self-admiration, and its unrealistic description of the boy carrying to Santiago's boat the harpoon, the gaff, and three-fourths of a mile of fishing line, which must have been too heavy for the boy (1967, 274).

In 1968, Claire Rosenfield acknowledges the folktale and mythic elements in the novella's theme of a tribal hero's confrontation with an oversized monster of the sea, whom the hero admires and fears.

She argues that the references to baseball "tend to fuse and confuse a way of life with a triode of entertainment", that Hemingway's old man has a banal range of perceptions, and that Hemingway's "emphatically male bias makes the purposive mingling of game and rite ridiculous" because baseball lacks all suggestion of cult participation or identification (51).

Jackson J. Benson opines that "Santiago becomes a figure too removed, almost precious in his highly stylized role, and his tragedy, with very carefully contrived suggestive detail in its proper orbit, lacks the spontaneity of moving passion." He claims that "the fish is a violation of the poetic terms of the allegory" and that "art is brought to the edge of the ridiculous by its very artfulness" (171, 172, 180).

1970s saw the publication of essays on *The Old Man and the Sea* like the studies of the biblical and baseball allusions by Joseph H. Flora and George Monteiro and the study of the novella as a lyric novel of organic unity by Linda Wagner.

Ben Stoltzfus's 1978 rereading of the Christological allusions in his chapter "Hemingway's Battle with God", is ingenious and interesting. He finds the Christological imagery essentially "non-Christian" and the novella a celebration "of pride rather than humility". His Lacanian interpretation of *The Old Man and the Sea,* focuses on three categories in exploring the submerged seven-eighths of the iceberg: (1) What Hemingway consciously put into the text, (2) What the reader puts into it in order to generate meaning, and (3) Hemingway's unconscious desire, which escapes his cognition but which is unveiled by a Lacanian reading.

Through diagrams of signifier, signified and referent, he demonstrates how metonymical slippage works. If DiMaggio has a spur and if a fighting cock has a spur, both are champions performing to the death. The marlin's spear resembles a baseball bat; the marlin fights to the death, and, like DiMaggio and the cock, is a champion; but since Santiago triumphs over the marlin, he is a greater champion. Again, through similar diagrams, he shows how Santiago's dreams of a pride of lions refers to his own pride and his own being a lion among fishermen. Thus when he brings the marlin to the shore, his identity is restored in the eyes of the other fishermen. The first object of desire, according to Lacan, is to be recognized by others.

Ben Stoltzfus gives a brief exposition of the Lacanian theory, which he uses as the framework for his interpretation of *The Old Man and the Sea*.

Kathlene Morgan and Luis Losada, in their essay, "Santiago in *The Old Man and the Sea*: A Homeric Hero", discuss the similarities Santiago shares with the heroic figures of *The Iliad* and *The Odyssey*. They refer to the Homeric heroes being born to their destinies like Achilles talking of his twin destinies, and point out that Santiago also claims that he is doing that which he was born for. Basic to the identity of the Homeric heroes is the belief that they are the best. Santiago is also the best. The authors find parallels between the Greek hero's respect and empathy for his Trojan enemies and Santiago's empathy for the marlin and the *dentuso*. They draw our attention to many other parallels, like the victor's fight to keep the body of the slain enemy, and the hero's prayers in the heat of the battle, and their challenges, threats, and vows of victory.

The authors trace similarities between the openings of *The Odyssey* and *The Old Man and the Sea.* In respect of the physical descriptions of Odysseus and Santiago—their skill, intelligence and wisdom, and also point out the repetition of words like 'suffer', 'suffering(s)' and 'endure' recurring over and over.

Chaman Nahal, in his book, *The Narrative Pattern in Ernest Hemingway's Fiction* discovers two modes of action—the systolic or the active action and the diastolic or the passive action in each fictional work of Hemingway, long or short. He traces this systolic-diastolic pattern in *The Old Man and the Sea* also and demonstrates how the Hemingway hero acts and pauses and acts again. During the diastolic period the hero returns to a deep mystery within himself through passivity and makes himself ready for next systolic move. Thus he is in touch with the rhythm of total life. He analyses *The Old Man and the Sea* in the light of this rhythm of life.

Interestingly, Chaman Nahal seems to be inspired by Carlos Baker's use of the image of systolic-diastolic action to describe the wave like operation of bracing and relaxation (the boy bracing and the lions relaxing) in *The Old Man and the Sea*, in his *Hemingway: The Writer as Artist.*

In my book-length work on Hemingway, *Ernest Hemingway: A Study in Narrative Technique*, I have analyzed Hemingway's narrative technique with a special reference to its change after the publication of *Green Hills of Africa* in the light of his total contrapuntal theme. After the African safari and the publication of *Green Hills of Africa*, Hemingway's theme of the lonely individual's personal efforts and tribulations of the first three novels yields place to teamwork and solidarity. Erotic and selfish love with its agony and ecstasy yields place to agape or love for all which involves giving rather than taking. Irony, which is the dominant figure of speech and the general tone of the first two novels is shown as slowly fading in the third novel and replaced by paradox in the last three novels of his life. This also explains the Christological elements and symbols in *For Whom the Bell Tolls, Across the River and into the Trees*, and *The Old Man and the Sea*, as paradox is an important characteristic of Jesus Christ's utterances. The compactness of the first two novels yields place to the complexity of form in the later novels. The first-person narration with its preoccupation with the protagonist's self and problems changes into the omniscient third-person narration in which there is, however, a sharp focus on the consciousness of the protagonist. *The Old Man and the Sea* telescopes the compactness and intensity of the early novels as well as the complexity of the later novels. The paradox that governs this novel is the transmutation of material failure into moral and spiritual triumph showing the protagonist suffering a victorious defeat.

Nageswara Rao, in his study of Hemingway's rhetoric, discusses his stylistic practices such as verbal irony, figurative language, repetition of motifs, and other devices. He demonstrates how Hemingway communicates his vision and influences our thinking about it through several forms of verbal irony such as parody, sarcasm and, understatement with suitable illustrations.

A feminist study of the novella by Martin Swan appeared in France in 1984, in which the misogyny in the novella in treatment of its four female characters—the female tourist, Santiago's wife, the sea, and the Portuguese man-of-war—is underlined.

Kenneth Lynn's 1987 biography of Hemingway has this ironic passage debunking *The Old Man and the Sea*:

> Today, there is only one question worth asking about *The Old Man.* How could a book that lapses repeatedly into lachrymose sentimentality and is relentlessly pseudo-biblical, that mixes cute talk about baseball ("I fear both the Tigers of Detroit and the Indians of Cleveland") with crucifixion symbolism of the most appalling crudity ("he slept face down on the newspapers with his arms out straight and the palms of his hands up"), have evoked such a storm of applause from neighbours and middle brows alike—and in such overwhelming numbers? (566).

Hemingway's third son, Gregory Hemingway's, contemptuous dismissal of the novella as "sickly a bucket of sentimental shop as was ever scrubbed off the bar-room floor" is cited in Lynn's biography (563).

Gerry Brenner, in his study of *The Old Man and the Sea* discovers that there is nothing great or extraordinary about Santiago, who is an ordinary person. He points out personal anxieties as a son and as a father, which contributed to the creation of Santiago. Brenner says that Hemingway's projection of himself into Santiago—a papa image—"reveals an anxiety that he himself is not the man he thinks Santiago is and the wish that he were." His parental neglect of his three sons and the consequent loss of influence over them results in Santiago wishing "that the boy were here" (98-99).

In an interesting and insightful approach, Priyadarshi Patnaik applies the *Rasa* Theory of Indian Aesthetics to the novella. *Rasa* is the basic human emotion transmuted into an aesthetic emotion. Patnaik looks at the novel from the point of view of *Vira Rasa* (the heroic *rasa*), the basic emotion for which is *utsaha* (energy), and its culmination in *Adbhuta Rasa* (wonder). All *rasas* lead ultimately to *Santha Rasa* (peace or tranquility), which is the restoration of the cosmic or moral order. Patnaik demonstrates in his essay that the old man fights with the marlin and the sharks heroically, making us wonder at his valour and endurance, and, in the end, transcends ordinary emotions and achieves *Santha Rasa* or tranquility and equilibrium (188-205).

12

A Note on the Conclusion of *The Old Man and the Sea*

What happens to Santiago in the end? This is a question in everybody's mind on reading the novella. Does Santiago die in the end?

After the last shark of the pack rolled away, Santiago had a serious breathing problem and felt a strange coppery taste in the mouth and was afraid for a while:

> He spat into the ocean and said, 'Eat that galanos. And make a dream you've killed a man.' (107)

This gives us the impression that he might die. The author seems to have planned the death of the dear old man. But as we follow the old man climbing up to his shack with the mast on his shoulder and reach the last paragraph of the novella, we find him not only alive but sleeping and dreaming about the lions:

> Up the road, in his shack, the old man was sleeping again. He was still sleeping on his face and the boy was sitting by him watching him. The old man was dreaming about the lions. (114)

What led Hemingway to change his plans for the old man? Mary Hemingway claims to have pulled off a coup and induced her tough writer-husband to tailor the conclusion of the novel after her heart's desire. Here is her account of how it all happened as narrated in *How It Was:*

> As the holidays ended, Ernest set out by himself on a new adventure, a story about an old Cuban fisherman he had put on the tape recorder inside his head years before and had sketched in a piece *Esquire* published in April 1936. This was happy work. Every morning he unwound a bit of the tape, the words falling smoothly onto the paper in his battered Royal portable, with none of the problems of disciplining turbulent emotions rephrasing meannesses, smoothing roughnesses that had so troubled him in the writing of *Across the River*. Every evening after supper when our guests had retired and the house was quiet I read the manuscript, beginning each time at the first page.... (283)

Mary Hemingway read the manuscript each night as the writing was in progress and developed great tension fearing for the old man's life as if he were someone very dear. This is how she tells her story:

> I had not found time before the Scribners arrived to tap out a neat copy and carbon of the old fisherman Santiago's story, but I had read it as before the Florida interlude, every evening from the first sentence until the last of that day's work. Every night the simple story gave me goose pimples I could not control. Ernest would touch my arm and smile, murmuring, "I did okay today, mmmm?" To him the goose flesh was proof positive that the quality of his work was good. I could never have manufactured the little bumps.
>
> But as the end of the story approached and Santiago had clubbed the sharks which had eaten half his great fish, I sensed something more than the tragedy of the fish.
>
> "Darling, I feel something ominous. Something bad is going to happen."
>
> "Maybe. I don't know."
>
> "Oh, lamb, you're not," said I divining.
>
> "You're not going to let this old man die. Please."
>
> "Maybe better for him."

> "How can you say that? He's old. But he's healthy, basically. He's brave and he's good. Please let him live."
>
> "I'm glad you like him so much."
>
> "I'll bet everybody would be happier if you let him alive."
>
> Ernest mumbled something.
>
> A few nights later when I read the last lines of the story, my goose pimples sprouted again.
>
> "Up the road, in his shack, the old man was sleeping again. He was still sleeping on his face and the boy was sitting by him watching him. The old man was dreaming about the lions." (286)

Mary Hemingway liked Santiago so much that she pleaded with her husband to "let him live". Hemingway seems to have conceded her request in a veiled, artistic way, taking care not to offend the aesthetic requirements of the story. This probably, was the reason for his pencil insertion, "'But there was not much of it'", (190-1:109) in the first draft of the novella, after telling us that 'the old man could hardly breathe and felt a strange taste in his mouth.'" It was coppery and sweet and he was afraid of it for a moment. *But there was not much of it* (emphasis is mine). Besides, Santiago's words to the sharks, "and make a dream you've killed a man" are significant in that the sharks did not kill Santiago but could only make a dream to that effect (emphasis mine).

When the boy went out to bring food and the papers and some balm for the old man's hands he was crying; but, in the last lines of the novella, he is shown sitting by the old man and watching him. The sharks may not have made a dream that they killed a man, but the old man was dreaming about the lions when the novel closes. The lions are a symbol of energy reserves and relaxation for the old man and we can infer that he was getting replenishment of energy from his dreams. The fact that Manolin was no longer crying also testifies to the fact that Santiago was neither dead nor dying.

Another happy circumstance for the old man is subtly suggested towards the end of the novella. A woman in a party of tourists asks a waiter about the long backbone of the great marlin and the waiter tries to explain in Spanish, what happened far out in the sea: "Tiburon, the waiter said, 'Eshark.' He was meaning to explain what had happened." But the English speaking tourists jumped to the conclusion that the waiter meant the skeleton of a shark, creating an ironic gap between the information offered and the information received.

Still, the conscious artist that he is, Hemingway leaves the novella somewhat open-ended in that he does not say in so many words that the old man is not going to die in his sleep, but the suggestion that he is not going to die is very strong. The dialogue between Santiago and Manolin and the way the old man drank his coffee and his dream about the lions and his assurance to the boy that he knows how to care for his hands and his curiosity about what happened in his absence including the fish the boy caught, all suggest that he will live.

13

The Manuscripts of the Novella

Most of the Hemingway papers are preserved in John F. Kennedy Presidential Library, Boston (Massachusetts).

The Manuscripts of *The Old Man and the Sea* are in three drafts:

The first draft, straightaway typed out by Hemingway from January 12 to February 15, 1951, contains pencil corrections, some blue pencil corrections and markings, word count for each day's writing and dates of writing. This is marked in ink by Mary Hemingway as "E's copy". This is classified as 190.1 (Young/Mann 16A) by the curator of the Hemingway Room in John F. Kennedy Presidential Library.

The second draft was typed by Mary Hemingway. It is marked in Mary Hemingway's hand on the first page as "M's copy. First Type script. M." This is classified as 191 (Young/Mann 16B). Corrections are made in ink in this draft.

A Manila envelope is enclosed with the third draft and it contains the following:

1. One sheet bearing the title Book IV.
2. One sheet showing word count for the first twenty pages, the second twenty pages, the third twenty pages, the fourth twenty pages, and the last nineteen pages.

Book IV might refer to Hemingway's plan of writing 'a sea novel' with 'the old man' as part of it.

THE FIRST DRAFT OF *THE OLD MAN AND THE SEA*

As a Senior Fulbright/ACLS visiting scholar and Adjunct

Professor of English in the University of Massachusetts, Boston, I had the opportunity of studying the first drafts and the revisions in the subsequent drafts of Hemingway's major fiction in the John F. Kennedy Presidential Library, Boston, The H.R.C. Library, Austin [Texas], the Bancroft Library, Chicago, the Library of Congress, Washington DC., and the New York Public Library in 1981-82, and in 1993.

The first draft of what we know today as *The Old Man and the Sea* provides incontrovertible evidence that it was straightway typed out, for we see the author thinking and noting in the margin and typing e.g. the marginal note: "Put in the small migratory birds and hawks. Put in the contest of rowing and the one of putting the hand down. Put in Casablanca" (190/1).

Hemingway's characteristic spelling ('loveing', 'moveing' etc.) and typing and his occasional doubt whether the spelling of a word is right also prove that the typescript is his first draft.

Contrary to his usual practice of revising his manuscripts again and again, either pruning or inserting passages, we find very few changes in the first two typescripts, which impresses us that the novella is an inspired work of art.

THE MAGIC 'BOX'

Hemingway makes a marginal note in the first draft (191:16): "Correct box to basquet" (sic), but, in the printed text, 'box' is retained. This 'box' eluded the notice of the author, the editor, and the printer (10-11). Is it a box or a basket? The box appears to be the author's and the basket Santiago's.

Is this box of coiled lines an unconscious symbol for the novel itself ? Or is it the box of the artist's hypnotic tricks of coiled lines with which he binds the reader even as he harpoons and lashes the marlin to his skiff?

In spite of Hemingway's intention to correct it as basket, this box persists weaving its magic on the reading public for more than half a century now.

14

The Old Man and the Sea on the Screen

Hemingway hated Hollywood's adaptations of his films and generally refused to see them. He is reported by Gene D. Phillips to have said:

> The best way for a writer to deal with Hollywood was to arrange a rendezvous with the movie men at the California State line. You throw your book, they throw you the money, then you jump into your car and drive like hell the way you came. (6)

Hemingway worked closely with his friend and film-maker, Leland Hayward, in an attempt to catch a live marlin off the coast of Cuba and Peru for the film on *The Old Man*. He also taught the scriptwriter, Peter Viertel, the minutiae of fishing. All that ended in an overweight Spencer Tracy cast as Santiago, with a banker's son cast as the boy, with a rubber fish, and Tracy floating for hours on end in a studio pond, talking to himself.

Hemingway must have been sorely disappointed with the movie-version of his novella. Already unhappy about the other movies made out of his novels and stories, he made furious outbursts. But the movie-makers had a big problem finding powerful visual equivalent for his remarkable prose. The other challenge is to translate the drama and tensions he creates, through his magic narrative, into cinematic equivalent. Linda Dittmar shows this problem as follows:

> As the fish nibbles on the bait, way down in the deep, Santiago fingers the line *softly, lightly and delicately....* Nibbling gently, turning away, and returning for more, the marlin is felt but never seen. This protracted anticipation ends suddenly, in a mixture of wonder, relief and uneasiness: when Santiago finally pulls at the line, the fish won't budge. In the film, this scene yields a powerful statement. Tracy pulls energetically, loud music underscores his effort with conspicuous silence next accompanying the fish's refusal to come up. Here is audio-visual drama however crude. But the film cannot depict invisible drama. The touch of rope against skin and all that it conveys gets lost. The thrill of promise, with the holding of action, the anticipation and possibility of fulfillment, are lost. Instead, the film rushes through the episode with Tracy dashing about in a flurry of activity that belies the text's mounting tension. (122)

Linda Dittmar points out that a resonant sense of verbal possibilities and meanings called forth in response from "the uncharted realms of the reader's imagination" is central to this passage describing the marlin taking the bait.

A writer like Hemingway, whose aesthetic principles are anchored to experience and reality poses a challenge to the movie-maker. In his *Time* interview, he says: "...I tried to make a real old man, a real boy, a real sea and a real fish and real sharks" (72). Naturally, when the movie was made and there was nothing real in it he was upset and reported to have remarked: "No picture with a f-ing rubber fish ever made a dime." Hemingway did not know, at that time, that a rubber fish would make waves and millions in a movie called "Jaws" a few decades later.

There are nuances in a text which the writer's imagination can capture and communicate to the reader's imagination, but which cannot be communicated to the audience by movie-makers. There can never be a greater stage or screen than that in our mind and imagination.

15

Conclusion

Hemingway put so much of himself in Colonel Cantwell, the hero of *Across the River and into the Trees*, and in the novel itself that he thought the novel his best. He is reported by Harvey Breit as having said: "I have moved through arithmetic, through plane geometry and algebra, and now I am in calculus" (14). But the novel got a bad press and critics tore it to pieces. Hemingway might have been reminded of his *Esquire* article of 1936, "On Blue Water : A Gulf Stream Letter", in which an old Cuban fisherman harpooned a huge marlin and lashed it to the skiff, but the sharks attacked the marlin and ate most of it. The old man fought them out bravely and, when he was picked up, he was crying and half-crazy from his loss.

To Hemingway's hurt sensibilities, *Across the River and into the Trees* must have looked like the helpless marlin and the reviewers and critics like the brutal, blood-thirsty sharks. Thus the marlin of *The Old Man and the Sea* is Hemingway's *Across the River and into the Trees*, ruthlessly attacked by the shark-like critics.

The marlin seems to symbolize the big prize. Readers of Hemingway generally miss its flashback. In *To Have and Have Not*, Johnson and Harry try to catch a marlin, which eludes them. In his next novel, *For Whom the Bell Tolls*, This symbolic marlin is successfully hooked. In the next novel it is harpooned and lashed to the skiff and, in *The Old Man and the Sea*, it is brought home after a memorable battle with the sharks and the big prize, the Nobel Prize, is finally achieved. It is interesting to note that Hemingway identifies with the hero of each of his novels in some measure. The hero grows with Hemingway from "The Indian Camp" of *In Our Time* to *The Old Man and the Sea.*

Hemingway's contrapuntal theme of man versus the vastnesses of the world—the abiding earth or the everlasting sea—which he has kept in the background or used as a framework, finally confronts him and becomes the main subject of a novel in *The Old Man and the Sea*, making it sound like 'the old man versus the sea'.

His changing worldview prompted him to change his techniques also after the African safari and the publication of *Green Hills of Africa.* The theme of 'separate peace' yields place to involvement for a good cause and selfish sexual love to selfless all embracing love. The priest's theory of love as service and sacrifice in *A Farewell to Arms* is shown in action in the later novels. This necessitated a change from the first-person to the third-person point of view. Hemingway must have become acutely conscious of the limitations of the first-person method and the advantages of the third-person method. He answered one of John Atkin's questions, on this subject, as follows:

> When I wrote the first two novels, I had not learned to write in the third-person. The first-person gives you great intimacy in attempting to give a complete sense of experience to the reader. It is limited, however, and in the third-person the novelist can work in other people's heads and in other people's country. His range is greatly extended and so are his obligations. I prepared myself for writing in the third-person by the discipline of writing *Death in the Afternoon*, the short stories and especially the long short stories of 'The Short Happy Life of Francis Macomber' and 'The Snows of Kilimanjaro.' (72-73)

The third-person point of view enables the author to tell us many things, which Santiago does not know, in *The Old*

Man and the Sea. Thus when the old man does not know what has taken the bait, we already have the superior knowledge that it is a marlin one hundred fathoms down in the sea (34). Later, as Santiago looks at the marlin constantly to make sure that it is true, and is blissfully ignorant of the approaching Mako shark, we keep track of the movements of the shark as he comes up from deep down in the water, and swims fast and hard on the course of the skiff, sometimes losing the scent and picking it up again (89-90). The third-person omniscient narration gives us this superior knowledge. This superior point of view makes us aware of the tragic irony of Santiago who pities the flying fish and the birds. We know that neither marlin nor dolphin nor shark nor the flying fish nor the birds nor Santiago has any chance against the "one single, lasting thing—the stream".

Paradox replaces irony as the dominant motif in his later novels. Whatever irony is still used subserves the paradox expressed by the novel. Paradox is an important aspect of Jesus's utterances as in "whosoever shall seek to save his life, shall lose it; and whosoever shall lose his life shall preserve it" (St. Luke, 17:33) or "Everyone that exalteth himself shall be abased; and he that humbleth himself shall be exalted" (St. Luke, 18:14).

Santiago catches a giant marlin, after eighty-four days of unsuccessful fishing, only to lose most of it to the sharks. His great triumph is reduced to a miserable failure and he brings home only the skeleton of the magnificent fish. We are aware of the painful irony in this situation. But this irony is transformed into a paradox when we consider how the old man fights the sharks with an indomitable will and brings home his prize, though in a bad shape, realizes his 'hubris', and achieves true humility admitting to himself as well as to the boy, who is his window on the outside world, that he is beaten (107, 112). Material failure is transmuted into moral and spiritual triumph, and Santiago suffers a victorious defeat.

Santiago is exalted by humbling himself. If the visible prize that he brings home is the skeleton of the marlin, the invisible prize is humility, which is greater than the highest prize, even the Nobel Prize, and enhances the value of any prize or position.

This leads us to Jesus and Christianity and explains the Christological elements and symbolism in the novel. Beginning with the Terrace where many of the fishermen made fun of the old man but failed to make him angry (7), the Christological symbols can be seen during the old man's struggles with the marlin, e.g. "He settled comfortably against the wood and took his suffering as it came" (56) or "He lay against the worn wood of the bow and rested all that he could (66)", or "'Ay', he said aloud. There is no translation for this word and perhaps it is just a noise such as a man might make, involuntarily, feeling the nail go through his hands and into the wood" (96). The last of these is a clear crucifixion image with Santiago/marlin (I wish I was the fish,... [56]; "I do not care who kills who" [82]) likened to Jesus on the cross and the galanos likened to the Roman soldiers. Later, Santiago, climbing up to his shack with the mast across his shoulder and falling down on the way, is the very image of Jesus carrying the cross to Golgotha.

Inside the shack, a tired and humbled Santiago assumes a position, very much like that of Jesus on the cross, but face down "with his arms out straight and the palms of his hands up" (110).

Even if we are prejudiced against symbolic writing and reading between the lines, we still find that the story, by itself, has an absorbing interest and a powerful appeal. Sean O' Faolain (113) and Robert P. Weeks (15-16) refer to this quality of Hemingway's unobtrusive narrative art as being responsible for the charge, made by some critics, that he has no art. *The Old Man and the Sea* is the best example of Hemingway's unobtrusive art, which pleases the common reader as well as the enlightened critic.

Select Bibliography

PRIMARY WORKS

Ernest Hemingway. *In Our Time*. New York: Charles Scribner's Sons, 1930 (First Pub. 1925).

——. *The Torrents of Spring*. New York: Charles Scribner's Sons, 1926.

——. *The Sun Also Rises*. New York: Charles Scribner's Sons, 1926.

——. *Men without Women*. New York: Charles Scribner's Sons, 1927.

——. *A Farewell to Arms*. New York: Charles Scribner's Sons, 1929.

——. *Death in the Afternoon*. London: Jonathan Cape, 1963 (First Pub. 1932).

——. *Winner Take Nothing*. New York: Charles Scribner's Sons, 1933.

——. *Green Hills of Africa*. New York: Charles Scribner's Sons, 1935.

——. *To Have and Have Not*. New York: Charles Scribner's Sons, 1937.

——. *The Fifth Column and the First Forty Nine Stories*. New York: Charles Scribner's Sons, 1938.

——. *For Whom the Bell Tolls*. New York: Charles Scribner's Sons, 1940.

——. *Men at War*. New York: Crown Publishers, 1942.

——. *Across the River and into the Trees*. New York: Charles Scribner's Sons, 1950.

——. *The Old Man and the Sea*. Harmondsworth: Penguin Books Ltd. 1966 (First Pub. 1952).

——. *A Moveable Feast.* New York: Charles Scribner's Sons, 1964.

——. *Islands in the Stream.* New York: Charles Scribner's Sons, 1970.

——. *The Garden of Eden.* New York: Charles Scribner's Sons, 1986.

——. *True at First Light.* New York: Charles Scribner's Sons, 1999.

——. Manuscripts of *The Old Man and The Sea.* John F. Kennedy Presidential Library, Boston, Mass., 190/1. (Classification and Numbers by Jo August, curator of the Hemingway Room).

SECONDARY WORKS

Anderson, Charles R. "Hemingway's Other Style", *Critiques of Four Major Novels*, ed. Carlos Baker. New York: Charles Scribner's Sons, 1962.

Atkins, John. *The Art of Ernest Hemingway.* London: Spring Books, 1952.

Backman, Melvin. "The Matador and the Crucified", *Modern American Fiction*, ed. Walton Litz. New York: Oxford University Press.

Baker, Carlos. *Ernest Hemingway: The Writer As Artist.* Princeton: Princeton University Press, 1963 (First Pub. 1956).

——. *Ernest Hemingway: A Life Story.* New York: Charles Scribner's Sons, 1969.

——. Ed. *Ernest Hemingway: Critiques of Four Major Novels.* New York: Charles Scribner's Sons, 1962.

——. Ed. *Ernest Hemingway: Selected Letters*, 1917—1961. New York: Charles Scribner's Sons, 1981.

Bates, H.E. "Hemingway's Short Stories", *Hemingway and His Critics: An International Anthology,* ed. Carlos Baker. New York: Hill and Wang, 1966.

Warren, Beach Joseph. "Ernest Hemingway: The Aesthetics of

Simplicity", *American Fiction 1920—1940*. New York: Macmillan, 1941.

Sylvia, Beach. *Shakespeare and Company*. London: Faber and Faber, 1959.

Benson, Jackson J. *Hemingway: The Writer's Art of Self-defense*. Minneapolis: University of Minnesota Press, 1969.

Bhimsingh, Dahiya. *The Hero in Hemingway: A Study in Development*. New Delhi: Bahri, 1978.

Bluestone, George. *Novels into Films*. Berkeley: University of California Press, 1957.

Brenner, Gerry. *The Old Man and the Sea: Story of a Common Man*. New York: Twayne Publishers, 1991.

Harvey, Breit. "Talk with Mr. Hemingway". New York: *Times Book Review*, LV (September 17, 1950).

Brett-Smith, H.F.B., ed. *The Four Ages of Poetry*, *Shelley's Defence of Poetry*, *Browning's Essay on Shelley*. Oxford: Basil Blackwell, Macmillan III. Percy Reprints, 1953.

Brooks, Cleanth. "Man on His Moral Uppers", *The Hidden God: Studies in Hemingway, Faulkner, Yeats, Eliot, and Warren*. New Haven: Yale University Press, 1963.

Burgum, Edwin Berry. "Ernest Hemingway and the Psychology of the Lost Generation", *Ernest Hemingway: The Man and His Work*, ed. J.K.M. McCaffery. New York: The World Publishing Company, 1950.

Burhans, Clinton S. "*The Old Man and the Sea*: Hemingway's Tragic Vision of Man", *Hemingway and His Critics: An International Anthology*, ed. Carlos Baker. New York: Hill and Wang, 1966.

Campbell, Joseph. *The Hero with a Thousand Faces*. Princeton: Princeton University Press, 1968 (First Pub. 1949).

Carpenter, F.I. "Hemingway Achieves the Fifth Dimension", *Hemingway and His Critics: An International Anthology*, ed. Carlos Baker. New York: Hill and Wang, 1966.

Cowley, Malcolm. "Nightmare and Ritual in Hemingway", *Hemingway: A Collection of Critical Essays*, ed. Robert P. Weeks. Englewood Cliffs (N.J.): Prentice Hall, 1962.

Dittmar, Linda. "Exultation or Excess? Hemingway, the Author and Hemingway on Screen", *Ernest Hemingway Centennial Essays*, ed. E. Nageswara Rao. Delhi: Pencraft International, 2000, 112-24. (Text of the Keynote Address at a National Seminar on "Hemingway's Fiction on Film", American Studies Research Centre, Hyderabad, India, November 20-21, 1995).

Eastman, Max. "Bull in the Afternoon", *Ernest Hemingway: The Man and His Work*, ed. J.K.M. McCaffery. New York: The World Publishing Company, 1950.

Edel, Leon. "The Art of Evasion", *Hemingway: A Collection of Critical Essays*, ed. Robert P. Weeks, Englewood Cliffs (NJ): Prentice Hall, 1962.

Eliot, T.S. *The Sacred Wood: Essays on Poetry and Criticism*. London: Methuen & Co., 1950 (First Pub 1920).

Fenton, Charles. *The Apprenticeship of Ernest Hemingway: The Early Years*. New York: The New American Library, 1961 (First Pub. 1954).

Flora, Joseph H. "Biblical Allusions in *The Old Man and the Sea*," *Studies in Short Fiction* 10 (1973), (143-147).

Frohock, W.M. *The Novel of Violence in America*. Boston: Beacon Press, 1964.

Ganzel, Dewey. "*Cabestro* and *Vaquilla*: The Symbolic Structure of *The Sun Also Rises*". *Sewance Review*, LXXVI (Jan-Mar., 1968).

Gurko, Leo. "*The Old Man and the Sea*", *College English*, 17 (October, 1955).

Halliday, E.M. "Hemingway's Ambiguity: Symbolism and Irony", *Interpretations of American Literature*, ed. Charles Feidelson, Jr. and Paul Brodtkorb, Jr. New York: Oxford University Press, 1959.

Harada, Keiichi. "The Marlin and the Shark: A Note on *The Old Man and the Sea*", *Hemingway and His Critics: An International Anthology*, ed. Carlos Baker. New York: Hill and Wang, 1966.

Hemingway, Mary Welsh. *How It Was*. New York: Alfred A. Knopf, 1976.

Hemingway, Leicester. *My Brother: Ernest Hemingway*. London: Weidenfield and Nicolson, 1962.

Hotchner, A.E. *Papa Hemingway*. New York: Random House, 1966.

Hurley, C. Harold. "Just 'a Boy' or 'Already a Man?': Manolin's Age in *The Old Man and the Sea*", *The Hemingway Review*, X, 2 (Spring 1991).

Killinger, John. *Hemingway and the Dead Gods: A Study in Existentialism*. Kentucky: University of Kentucky Press, 1960.

Levin, Harry. "Observations on the Style of Ernest Hemingway", *Kenyon Review*, XIII (Autumn 1951).

Lewis, Robert W. *Hemingway on Love*. Austin & London: University of Texas, 1965.

Lodge, David. *Language of Fiction: Essays in Criticism and Verbal Analysis of the English Novel*. London: Routledge and Kegan Paul, 1966.

Macleish, Archibald. "Ernest Hemingway", *Time,* LXIV (Dccember 13, 1964).

Maurois, Andre. "Ernest Hemingway", *Hemingway and His Critics: An International Anthology,* ed. Carlos Baker. New York: Hill and Wang, 1966.

Meloney, Michael F. "Ernest Hemingway: The Missing Third Dimension", *Hemingway and His Critics: An International Anthology*, ed. Carlos Baker. New York: Hill and Wang, 1966.

Monteiro, George. "Santiago, DiMaggio, and Hemingway: The Ageing Professionals of *The Old Man and the Sea*", *Fitzgerald/Hemingway Annual* 1975, ed. Mathew J. Bruccoli and C.E. Frazer Clark, Jr. Englewood, Col.; Information Handling Services, 1975, 273-80.

Morgan, Kathleen and Luis Losada "Santiago in *The Old Man and the Sea:* A Homeric Hero", *The Hemingway Review,* Vol. 12. No. 1, Fall 1992.

Morris, Wright. *The Territory Ahead*. New York: Atheneum, 1963.

Nahal, Chaman. *The Narrative Pattern in Ernest Hemingway's Fiction*. Delhi: Vikas, 1977.

Rao, Nageswara E. *Ernest Hemingway: A Study of His Rhetoric*. New Delhi: Arnold Heinemann, 1983.

O'Faolain, San. "A Clean Well-Lighted Place", *Hemingway: A Collection of Critical Essay*, ed. Robert P. Weeks. Englewood Cliffs (N.J.): Prentice Hall, 1962.

Patnaik, Priyadarshi. "*The Old Man and the Sea* in the Light of Rasa Theory: An Indian Reading of Hemingway", *The Ernest Hemingway Companion*, ed. Somdatta Mandal. Kolkata: SAS Enterprise, 2002.

Phillips, Gene D. *Hemingway and Film*. New York: Frederick Ungar Publishing Company, 1980.

Plimpton, George. "An Interview with Ernest Hemingway", *Hemingway and His Critics: An International Anthology*, ed. Carlos Baker. New York: Hill and Wang, 1966.

Rao, P.G. Rama. *Ernest Hemingway: A Study in Narrative Technique*. Delhi: S. Chand & Company, 1980.

Rosenfield, Claire. "New World, Old Myths", *Twentieth Century Interpretations of The Old Man and the Sea: A Collection of Critical Essays*, ed. Katharine T. Jobes. Englewood Cliffs (N.J.): Prentice Hall, 1968.

Ross, Lilian. "How Do You Like It Now, Gentlemen?" *Hemingway: A Collection of Critical Essays*, ed. Robert P. Weeks. Englewood Cliffs (N.J.): Prentice Hall, 1962.

Rovit, Earl. *Ernest Hemingway*. Boston: Twayne, 1963.

Sanderson, Stewart. *Ernest Hemingway*. Edinburgh: Oliver and Boyd Ltd., 1961.

Schorer, Mark. "With Grace Under Pressure", *Ernest Hemingway: Critiques of Four Major Novels*, ed. Carlos Baker. New York: Charles Scribner's Sons, 1962.

Stein, Gertrude. *The Autobiography of Alice B. Toklas*. New York: Vintage Books, 1961 (First Pub. 1933).

Stoltzfus, Ben. *Gide and Hemingway: Rebels against God.* Port Washington, New York: Kennikat Press, 1978, 43, 44, 47.

——. "*The Old Man and the Sea:* A Lacanian Reading", *Hemingway: Essays of Re-Assessment*, ed. Frank Scaffela. New York: Oxford University Press, 1991, 190-99.

Swan, Martin "*The Old Man and the Sea*: Women Taken for Granted", *Visages de la feminite*, ed. A.J. Bullier and J.M. Recault. St. Denis, France: Université de Reunion, 1984, 147-63.

Sylvester, Bickford. "Hemingway's Extended Vision: *The Old Man and the Sea.*" PMLA, LXXXI (March 1966).

——. "They Went Through This Fiction Everyday: Informed Illusion in *The Old Man and the Sea*", *Modern Fiction Studies, XII* (Winter 1966-67).

Tanner, Tony. *The Reign of Wonder: Naivety and Reality in American Literature.* Cambridge: Cambridge University Press, 1965.

Wagner, Linda. "The Poem of Santiago and Manolin", *Modern Fiction Studies*, 19 (1973-74), 517-29.

Waldmeir, Joseph. "Confiteor Hominem: Ernest Hemingway's Religion of Man", *Hemingway: A Collection of Critical Essays,* ed. Robert P. Weeks. Englewood Cliffs (N.J): Prentice Hall, 1962.

Warren, Robert Penn. "Introduction", *A Farewell to Arms.* New York: Charles Scribner's Sons, 1957. (First Pub. 1929).

Weeks, Robert P. "Fakery in *The Old Man and the Sea*", *College English,* 24 (December 1962), 182-92.

Welland, D.S.R. "Hemingway's English Reputation", *The Literary Reputation of Hemingway in Europe*, ed. Roger Asselineau. New York: New York University Press, 1965.

Wells, Arvin S. "A Ritual of Transfiguration: *The Old Man and the Sea*", *University Review* 30 (Winter 1963).

White, William. Ed. *By-Line: Ernest Hemingway: Selected Articles and Dispatches of Four Decades.* New York: Charles Scribner's Sons, 1967.

Williams, Wirt. *The Tragic Art of Ernest Hemingway.* Baton Rouge: Louisiana State University Press, 1981.

Wilson, Edmund. *Axel's Castle: A Study in the Imaginative Litertaure* of 1870—1930. New York: Charles Scribner's Sons,1950.

——. "The Emergence of Ernest Hemingway", *Hemingway and His Critics: An International Anthology*, ed. Carlos Baker. New York: Hill and Wang, 1966.

——. "Introduction", *In Our Time.* New York: Charles Scribner's Sons, 1930.

Young, Philip. "Hemingway: A Defense", *Hemingway: A Collection of Critical Essays*, ed. Robert P. Weeks Englewood Cliffs (N.J.): Prentice Hall, 1962.

——. *Ernest Hemingway: A Reconsideration.* University Park: Pennsylvania University Press, 1966.

Index